REAL WINNING

REAL WINNING

FAITH IN THE LIVES OF THIRTEEN GREAT ATHLETES

Carlton Stowers

WORD BOOKS
PUBLISHER
WACO, TEXAS

A DIVISION OF
WORD, INCORPORATED

Library of Congress Cataloging-in-Publication Data

Stowers, Carlton.
  Real winning.

  1. Athletes—United States—Biography. 2. Sports—Religious aspects. I. Title.
GV697.A1S753 1986   796'.092'2 [B]   86–9208
ISBN 0–8499–3054–5

Printed in the United States of America

67898 FG 987654321

For
Jerry and Gayle Curnutt
the remarkably inspiring parents
of the young man in chapter twelve . . .

Contents

For whatever is born of God overcomes the world; and this is the victory that overcomes the world, our faith.
Who is it that overcomes the world
  but he who believes that Jesus is the Son of God?

1 JOHN 5:4–5, RSV

REAL
WINNING

Preface

THE AMOUNT OF LABOR it has taken for this book to make the transition from idea to printed page, frankly, has been far greater than I had ever expected. On first thought, it seemed that the most demanding problem would be the decision of whom to profile and whom to leave for perhaps another book along the same lines at some future date. I strongly feel there are certainly plenty of candidates for a book of this type. What one generally does is to make a list of the candidates, trim it to a workable length, do the interviews, and get on with the business of writing. Sounds simple, right?

This was hardly the case. Never, in my innumerable trips to the typewriter to prepare a book-length manuscript, have I struggled so. Not that the writing was difficult; nor was the subject matter a problem. Quite the contrary! The people profiled herein are among the most interesting subjects I've ever dealt with.

My problem was not my subject matter but, rather, the manner in which I would approach it. As one of those who holds to the old-time philosophy that people need role models— for heroes—I decided that, if possible, I would attempt to make this book something more than a celebration of athletic achievement. Super Bowls and World Series and incredible records are, admittedly, fun to write about. I have long held that the athletic arena promises high drama and suspense that no courtroom, business meeting, or political rally can match.

Headline-making athletic accomplishment, however, wasn't

all I was looking for. I wanted those included in this book to be people who not only have rubbed the touchstone of celebrity status but who have also endured the day-to-day woes and frustrations that are part of life's journey. I've also included the story of a young man who, through a bizarre twist of fate, was robbed of his chance to earn his measure of glory. (The story of Kevin Curnutt first appeared in *D* magazine, and I appreciate their permission to allow it to be included in this collection.)

The people you will meet in this book are real; some are not greatly unlike you and me. Most important, they are people who have called on God for help, have admitted their own failings, and have worked to rebound from setbacks. They are people who have demonstrated a courage that goes far and beyond that needed on the field of athletic competition. This courage is demonstrated in their willingness to admit their personal failures, in their willingness to accept blame for detours down the wrong roads, and in their efforts put forth to regain precious things lost.

There is another admission I must make before we proceed. As a journalist who has spent a great deal of time in pressboxes, in locker rooms, and on the sidelines, I have watched a change in the manner in which those in my profession deal with today's athlete. Time was—in what some elder statesmen like to refer to as the "Golden Age of Sports"—when the sportswriter's job was only to glorify the achievements of those who hit the game-winning home run or scored the winning touchdown. If the athlete drank to excess, was hooked on drugs, or had financial problems, it was his business and not that of the person reading the morning paper.

Today, however, an athlete's life is no longer his own. He now holds rank right up there with politicans and movie stars. If he's got tax problems, you're going to read about it. If his marriage is on the rocks, this fact will also find its way into the headlines. If he checks into a drug rehabilitation clinic or gets crossways with the IRS, it's a bigger story than any on-the-field accomplishment he might be credited with. Simply stated, it is part of the price now demanded of those who enjoy such public visibility.

I wonder, though, if we haven't ventured into the neighborhood of overkill. As a long-time follower of sports, I am bone-weary of reading about contract negotiations for celestial amounts, investigations of recruiting violations, gambling probes, player strikes, and confrontations between the law and athletes. More and more, I find myself wondering if the "sport" has, in fact, gone out of sport.

Maybe I made the mistake of getting too close. If it is a criminal admission of shoddy journalism to note that I have not been among those racing to look under the sports world's next rock, hoping to uncover a blockbuster scandal, then I stand guilty. But I am not so naive as to ignore the fact that there is a valid reason for exposing that which causes the rotting of public interest. I don't want my kids growing up idolizing some guy who hits .350, but goes home at night and gets drunk and beats his wife. At the same time, I don't want them to think that those few athletes who are less than exemplary represent the entire sports spectrum.

I think this is why I labored so with this *Real Winning*. I wanted to write about people who represent something good in mankind as well as being men whose athletic reputation is well documented. What I finally decided on—as I think you will soon realize—is a chronicle of people who just happened to be outstanding athletes, men who have fought battles in everyday life. And the battles have been every bit as difficult as the games they have played so well.

This became the definition of *real winning* with which I chose to work. I hope what has resulted has been worth the labor. At the risk of sounding immodest, I like to think it is.

Jim Sundberg

Catcher, Kansas City Royals

IT WAS ONE OF THOSE marvelous, crisp autumn days that
Iowa sees occasionally during the month of October. Mother
Nature had turned the University of Iowa campus into a parade
of dazzling color; and there was an almost electric excitement
in the air as students and returning alumni mingled, anticipating

the homecoming football game scheduled for later in the day.

Across the campus, on the baseball diamond, coach Duane Banks was rushing the season a bit, staging an intrasquad game for the benefit of those former players who wanted an early preview of his team. For fun, he had invited some of them to stop by, put on a uniform, and play a few innings.

As the game progressed, Banks, obviously enjoying himself, rode the catcher unmercifully. When he connected for a double to left field, the coach cupped his hands to his mouth and roared, "Maybe you ought to get this guy to pitch to you every day. I bet you might even manage to hit your weight after a while."

Pulling up at second base, the hitter smiled. He had hit just .201 in the major leagues the season before. Banks' joking reference wasn't at all lost on him.

And when he was behind the plate, catching the enthusiastic young college pitchers, the coach repeatedly encouraged his base runners to try to steal. "Hey," Banks yelled, "everybody in the American League ran on this guy last year. No reason why you guys can't."

A few Iowa players tried stealing second base and were quickly thrown out by the strong-armed catcher, who had, during his ten-year major league career, been honored as one of the best in the business. He had earned six Golden Glove awards for his defensive play. He'd been selected to the Major League All-Star team. At one time, he had been generally regarded as the best catcher in the American League, maybe in all of professional baseball.

All of this was before the troubled season when his hitting fell off drastically, and his arm ached every time he attempted to deliver the ball to second base; this was all before his own manager criticized him publicly and finally announced he was being traded to the Milwaukee Brewers.

The season had been a new, unwelcomed experience for Jim Sundberg.

For a decade, Sundberg had been the cornerstone of a Texas Rangers franchise which seemed forever spinning its wheels. Good players had come and gone, managers had been hired and fired, front office decisions had made management look like a revolving door disaster, and those fans who did come to the ball park were often there only to cheer the opposition.

Jim Sundberg, however, was a different story. Clearly the fans' favorite in Arlington Stadium, he represented the quality and class that the baseball community had been yearning for from the day major league baseball came to the Dallas-Fort Worth area. Even in the worst of times, the fans knew they could count on Jim Sundberg. He was their diamond among the sand pebbles.

Not only was he a premier catcher but Sundberg represented the things in sports that fathers taking their wide-eyed young sons to the ball park wanted them to see and learn from. Jim Sundberg made no secret of his strong Christian beliefs. One usually critical Dallas newspaper columnist said, "Jim Sundberg is to the Texas Rangers what Roger Staubach was to the Dallas Cowboys."

For years, then, Jim Sundberg *was* the Texas Rangers to many fans. He represented their hope that one day the team might right itself and develop into a contender. There came a time when the annual voting for the year's favorite Ranger was but a formality. Everyone knew Jim Sundberg was going to win, even before the ballots were printed and distributed.

Then Doug Rader arrived, a tough-talking, hard-line manager who promised to shake things up and turn Texas from a dogpatch franchise into a contender. He was immediately critical of the players whom he greeted upon his arrival. One of his primary targets was, surprisingly, Jim Sundberg. Rader acknowledged that Jim had been an excellent player. But Sundberg was now "past his prime." It was time to seek a replacement, a new face. For the next two years, Rader made no secret of the fact that he hoped to trade Sundberg as quickly as possible.

At the 1983 winter baseball meetings, the Rangers finally struck a deal that sent Sundberg to Milwaukee in exchange for a twenty-three-year-old backup catcher and a pitcher, who had failed to even post a winning record in Class A ball. Obviously, it was a slap in the face to Sundberg.

The media, aware of the strained relationship between Rader and his former catcher, gave Sundberg every opportunity to level a parting blast. Admittedly frustrated and disappointed by the turn of events, Sundberg was restrained.

"I had a poor season last year," he said as he received news of his trade. "I'm the one accountable for that. But I can come back. I'm just not a player who is motivated by intimidation and hind-kicking. I've been around too long for that. The Texas Rangers are the team I broke in with, and they have been a big part of my life. I will miss being a part of the organization. But things work out for a reason. What I plan to do is look ahead and find out what the future holds."

This was the public declaration of Jim Sundberg. Privately, he was at an all-time low. Physically, he felt he had several good years remaining in him as a major league catcher. Mentally, he wondered if he could ever recapture the enthusiasm he once held for the game.

Since the time he was called to Texas from Class AA Pittsfield in 1974, he had approached the game with boyish enthusiasm. He had caught more games per season than any other catcher in the majors, rarely asking for a day off to rest aching knees or a sore arm. For the Rangers to win, he knew, it was necessary for him to be in the lineup. Though many of his peers warned him that he might shorten his career by insisting on playing every day, Sundberg played regularly—because he loved the game and felt his contribution was needed. (He still holds the American League record for most games caught in a single season—155 for the Rangers in 1975.)

Then suddenly, Rader, for reasons Jim never completely understood, began the endless stream of criticisms. Sundberg's input about the Rangers' pitching staff was no longer asked for. The leadership that he had for years tried to provide apparently wasn't wanted. The man whom the franchise had picked in the second round of the 1973 draft was no longer needed.

Thus, when the news came to him that he had been traded to the Brewers, he told his wife, Janet, he was concerned he might never recapture his old enthusiasm for the game.

But all of this changed that day during the intrasquad game on the Iowa campus. The good-natured ribbing from his old college coach, the enthusiasm he saw on the faces of the young collegians preparing for their season, rubbed off. Suddenly, performing before a handful of spectators in a meaningless nongame, Jim Sundberg realized he was again eager to play.

"I don't know when I've had so much fun," he said later. "It was great. Out there, playing with those guys, there was no management to deal with—no owners, no criticism, no press.

It was just baseball, and it was fun. It dawned on me that I had forgotten about that part of the game. I'd been so wrapped up in all the deal-making and trade rumors and such that I had forgotten why I was there in the first place. I'm a ball player, period. I decided I would focus on that and let the other business take care of itself.

"That Saturday on the campus of the University of Iowa, I realized that I still wanted to play."

Jim Sundberg grew up in Galesburg, Illinois, the son of a mail carrier, who, at an early date, planted the idea in Jim's mind of his one day becoming a major league baseball player. Sundberg's father would return from his route daily and accompany his son to a nearby park, where he would pitch to him until darkness forced them to return home to a warmed-over dinner.

"All I thought about in those days was baseball," Jim recalls. "But I didn't have the confidence in myself that my father did. I was playing the game for the fun of it, trying to be the best I could. He wasn't one of those pushy Little League fathers—not by any stretch. But he saw my enthusiasm and encouraged it. I don't really know that he was perceptive enough to see that I had the potential to play professionally, but urged me to set that as my goal."

By the time he graduated from high school, Sundberg was a draft pick of the Oakland A's. Jim and his father discussed the pro-ball opportunity but agreed that a college education and a few more years of athletic seasoning would be in his best interest.

Sundberg went off to the University of Iowa with more than an athletic scholarship and a big league potential. He took with him a faith in God that had been nurtured as carefully as his athletic talents.

"I'm fortunate that I was raised in a Christian environment," he says. "I'm not saying I was the kind of person God would have wanted me to be when I was younger, but my parents did provide me with the foundation of a Christian faith. They made sure that I attended church regularly, impressed upon me the importance of prayer, and were careful to take me down a notch or two when I got to thinking that my athletic accomplishments were more important than they should be."

It was, however, only after arriving in the major leagues

that Jim Sundberg realized sports and Christianity could work hand in hand. In Dallas, he had the opportunity to meet evangelist Bill Glass and inspirational speaker Zig Ziglar. On several occasions, he heard them speak of God's love and the positive effects of self-confidence. They were touching people's lives, Sundberg realized, and he felt a growing urge to do the same. Thrilling fans with a base hit or a good defensive play was exhilarating, but to reach others on a more personal level, he felt, would be even more rewarding.

Then one day when leaving the Arlington Stadium, Sundberg ran out of gas and was given a ride to a service station by a woman named Kathryn Byron. She later introduced Jim to her husband, and the couple invited the Sundbergs to services at the Pantago Baptist Church. A new world opened to the up-and-coming Rangers catcher.

"There were a great number of people who influenced me in those early days in Dallas," Jim recalls, "those who spoke to our baseball chapel meetings before games, the people at the church, men like Bill Glass and Zig Ziglar. I saw the wonderful things they were doing, the sharing of themselves in such a Christian way. And I knew I wanted to be a part of all that if I could."

The first step, he realized, was to be more open about his Christianity. "At first," he says, "there were guys on the team who kidded me a great deal, called me Billy Graham, things like that. But the commitment I felt ran so deep that it didn't bother me. I wanted to share the blessings and knew no other way than to witness wherever and whenever the opportunity presented itself."

Though he didn't press his beliefs on other players, Sundberg stood ready to talk with any who sought him out. He stood ready to witness to youth groups and to church gatherings. In time, he and his wife, Janet, began a Bible study for Rangers players and their families. At the initial meeting, only three of his teammates were present. But the number soon grew to a point where almost half the team was regularly attending, hearing the speakers whom the Sundbergs had invited to attend.

As Sundberg's faith grew, so did his baseball success. "I found that I was far more at peace with myself," he says. "There was a time when I went into every game I played tense and nervous. I was like a coiled spring, ready to come unwound. But as I grew spiritually, I relaxed more. And as I did, I sensed others on the team relaxing as well. Having completely turned my life over to God, I realized that all he expected from me was a maximum effort in those things I did with my life—and this applied to baseball as well. I continued to work hard, to prepare myself to do the best I could, then just relaxed and played the game."

It was this kind of attitude that earned him a place on the All-Star roster during the 1978 season. "Every major league ballplayer dreams of being picked to play in the All-Star Game," he says. "And I was thrilled. Looking back on it, though, I'd have to say the biggest thrill I had in connection with the game was being asked to deliver the opening prayer at the chapel meeting we had prior to the game."

Sundberg's Christian involvement also lent renewed strength to his family life. "We've grown together as Christians over the years," Janet says. "Our relationship has always been good, but it got even better as we became more and more active in the church and other religious activities."

It was this shared strength that enabled the Sundberg family to overcome the setbacks. "After I came to really believe and trust the Lord to guide my path," Jim says, "I realized that there is a reason, a purpose to everything. We were put to a test in 1981 when Janet lost a baby to a miscarriage in the eighth month of her pregnancy. It was a difficult time for us all, but we prayed for guidance and pulled together even more.

"If our faith in God hadn't been what it was, I doubt we would have had another child. But we were determined to try again." Just over two years ago, the third Sundberg child, daughter Briana, was born. "She's such a joy to everyone," Jim says. "She's really special to us. Aside from Janet, the kids [thirteen-year-old Aaron, nine-year-old Audra, and Briana] are the center of my universe."

In truth, there were times after leaving the Rangers when Jim Sundberg questioned his belief that he still had several good years left. Though he was given the starting catcher's job immediately upon his arrival in Milwaukee, a back injury soon sent him to the sidelines.

Again the rumor that he was nearing the end of his career

began to circulate. But he came back strong and eventually reclaimed the job and another berth on the All-Star team. Suddenly, Jim Sundberg felt back on top of his game, playing much as he had during his glory days with the Texas Rangers.

He knew, however, that his role with the Brewers was only that of a stop-gap performer. "I knew when I went there," he says, "that I was there just to fill in until their young catcher, Bill Schroeder, was ready to play every day. Initially, I felt it would be a couple of years, but when I was hurt and he got the opportunity to play—and played well—I knew my role would be diminished the next year."

When the club's general manager approached him after the season, asking how he would feel about catching only 90 (out of 162) games the next year, Sundberg knew he would have to move on. He had, after all, led the American League catchers in fielding and throwing out base stealers in 1984. Sundberg felt he should be catching regularly and asked that the Brewers trade him.

And, in an odd twist of fate, they began talking of a trade with the sagging Texas Rangers franchise, now far down in the standings and desperate to do something that might return fans to the ball park.

Since the Sundbergs still called Arlington, Texas, their home, the idea at first was inviting. "Janet liked the idea of our being settled again, not living half the year at our home there [in Arlington] and the other half somewhere else. But we both knew that some of the things that had happened in that last year I was with the Rangers had been unsettling. There was the fear of going back to that kind of atmosphere, seeing old wounds reopened. We talked about it a lot, and I even went down and talked with the Rangers. But it just didn't seem like the thing to do. We decided, instead, to see what other options were available."

Soon thereafter Sundberg became the property of the Kansas City Royals, the first team with legitimate world championship possibilities he'd ever been with. The move proved to be the beginning of the most exciting adventure of his athletic career.

There were times during the 1985 season, however, that were hardly an indication of what was to come. In August, Sundberg suffered torn cartilage in his left rib cage and was forced to sit out twenty-eight games. Slowly he worked himself back into peak condition, and, throughout the stretch drive portion of the season, Sundberg was a major factor in Kansas City's advancement toward the western division title. He was hitting the ball well, ending the regular season with a .245 batting average, thirty-five runs batted in and ten home runs, and he was working well behind the plate. The youthful Royals' pitching staff, in fact, collectively credited Sundberg with much of the success they enjoyed.

It was ten months after joining the Royals that he finally found himself in the role he had spent a lifetime dreaming about. The Royals and Toronto Bluejays had battled into the seventh and deciding game of their American League playoff series. For one, there would be a trip to the World Series; for the other, the long season would be ended.

The thirty-four-year-old Sundberg, who had never even been close to earning a championship ring during his lengthy and impressive career, lifted Kansas City into the Series in game seven with a bases-loaded triple.

"There are a lot of moments I'll remember," he says, "but that one has to be the highlight. Standing there at third base, knowing we were going to the World Series, brought back all those feelings about winning that I wasn't sure I still had."

Suddenly, the one-time castaway was the toast of the town. His heroics continued into the World Series as he scored the winning run in Kansas City's electrifying comeback win over the highly favored St. Louis Cardinals in the sixth game.

The Royals were one game away from elimination when Sundberg hit safely in the second inning and later advanced to second base. Teammate Buddy Biancalana then singled. Aware that his team needed something upon which to build momentum and confidence, Sundberg made the turn at third and, with a stunned crowd looking on, headed for home plate. To many of the pro-Cardinals fans in the stands that night, it appeared that St. Louis right fielder Cesar Cedeno's throw would beat Sundberg to the plate. At the last moment, however, Sundberg dove head first toward the plate, his hand catching the corner just a fraction of a second before rival catcher Tom Nieto was able to apply the tag.

Suddenly, the Royals were alive, leading the Cardinals by

a run! Before the inning was over, Willie Wilson increased the lead as he connected on a two-run triple with two outs. Longtime baseball followers will look back to that second inning surge, led by Sundberg's heroics, as the turning point of the Series.

So now, Jim Sundberg is the catcher for the defending world champion Kansas City Royals. Finally, after over a decade of sweat and frustration and extra hours in the batting cage, there is a championship ring on his finger. There are no rumors of trade, no whispers that he has grown too old or too slow to survive in the game he's enjoyed for twelve years.

Now he talks of playing for two, maybe three, more years. Jim would like to break Al Lopez's record of having caught 2,000 major league games (Sundberg has 1,620); and he'd like to relive the experience of a world championship. And, perhaps even more important than records or championships is the fact that he's still having fun.

"Sometimes," he says, "when things happen in your life, you aren't able to see what the final outcome will be for a while. I've had ups and downs, just like everyone else in this business, and there were times when I wasn't sure what they meant. But now, I'm thankful for everything that's happened to me in my baseball career. I'm fortunate that I had the opportunity to play ball in three different cities. Texas was a great place to play. Milwaukee was a great place to play. And Kansas City has been a gift, a reward, I think, for my faith and trust in God.

"I strongly feel that everything I have—my family, my friends, my baseball success—has come to me from above. And being an athlete has provided me with a platform from which to show my appreciation for what the Lord has done for me. So, no, I'm not still in the game just to win or improve my batting average or chase records. That's part of it, but the fact that it has allowed me the opportunity to share my faith with so many others is also very important. When people find out you're a Christian athlete, believe me, the news spreads like wildfire."

Particularly if you happen to also be a member of the reigning champions of major league baseball.

Joe Gibbs

Coach, Washington Redskins

THE OCCASION WAS A Bible study meeting at a place called the Triangle House, a home for disadvantaged teenagers in one of the less attractive sections of Washington, D.C. An enthusiastic speaker, looking considerably younger than his forty-three years, was addressing the predominantly black group.

"The most exciting days of my life," he said, "have been:

number one, the day I became a Christian; number two, the day I got married; and, number three, when my kids were born." Additionally, he spoke of the warmth and comfort his Christian beliefs had brought to his life, of the importance of setting personal goals, and of the strength God provides for those who pursue their ambitions.

There was no boasting, no recollections of his own noteworthy accomplishments. This was no "if you work hard and dedicate your lives, you can one day be important like me" speech. Rather, he talked of love and faith, determination and trust.

One of the youngsters in the audience had been attentively listening to the message and finally leaned in the direction of counselor Larry Jiggetts and whispered, "That dude looks really familiar. You know who he is?"

Jiggetts, more than a little amused, advised the youngster that he was listening to Joe Gibbs, head coach of the Washington Redskins (the team that just a few months earlier had won the first Super Bowl championship in the franchise's long history)— Joe Gibbs, the National Football League Coach of the Year.

"Man," the youngster said, "that's something. What's he doing down here talking to us?"

Gibbs was there because of a commitment he had made shortly after being named the Redskins coach prior to the 1981 season. Lending help to teenagers who had become wards of the court—homeless, truant, and in and out of trouble with the law—was a challenge Gibbs had accepted. He made the commitment even before he began to grapple with the pressures and responsibilities of being a head coach. Yet, it is one of the aspects of his life that the Monday morning sports pages seldom mention.

Joe Jackson Gibbs, son of a North Carolina sheriff, goes about the business of sharing his faith with the same dedication and enthusiasm he has for preparing his team for its weekly challenges.

"When I was an assistant coach in Tampa Bay," he says, "my church conducted a ministry with a local delinquents' home. I got involved and really enjoyed it. And I saw some positive things come from what we were trying to do. When I moved to Washington, I told myself that I wanted to get involved in something similar.

"One Sunday, during Sunday school, one of our members said he had some houses in the city and had contracted with an organization that was going to open them up to the teenagers. I told him of the program in Tampa Bay. He said he'd be more than willing to try some Bible study classes if anyone was willing to help. It was the answer to my prayers. We immediately began putting a plan together and making a list of people who would be willing to get involved."

In theory, the idea sounded good. But many of the counselors who had long been working with problem teenagers were skeptical. "I had a couple of them willing to bet me $1,000 that the classes wouldn't last more than two weeks," Gibbs said.

That was three years and hundreds of classes ago.

Still, there are few, outside the Triangle House organization, who are aware of Gibbs's involvement. He insists on and feels most comfortable with a low-keyed approach. He doesn't want to be introduced as Joe Gibbs, Coach of the Year. He doesn't wear his Super Bowl ring to the meetings. In a sense, he operates in two different worlds, where inhabitants of each know precious little about the other. At the Triangle House, his athletic accomplishments don't count for nearly as much as his obvious interest in a youthful segment of Washington's society (which hasn't had too many people interested in it).

"It has been very rewarding to me," Joe says. "There's something about getting to know teenagers that I particularly enjoy. The kids I've had the opportunity to get to know are sharp; they don't miss a thing. They just haven't had the chances that most of us have had.

"I can't begin to explain what the program has done for me. For instance, I remember a counselor telling me once about this kid who seldom showed up at the house and never took part in any activities. For some reason though, he did come to a couple of our Bible study meetings. He never said anything. But after a couple of times of just sitting and listening, he approached the counselor and told him, 'I'm trying to do the things they're talking about, but I'm having a hard time. What they're talking about isn't as easy as it sounds. But I'm trying.'

"How can that kind of effort not tug at your heart? What he was saying and learning was that being a Christian isn't an easy thing, and it takes a great deal of work."

The experiences of that particular youngster are very familiar to Joe Gibbs. His goals as a coach and as a Christian took
a long time to achieve. There were countless hard times and
blind alleys to be dealt with before he reached the place in life
he currently enjoys.

The long sought-after opportunity to serve as a head coach,
for instance, took seventeen frustrating years to present itself.
And, when it finally did, there were nagging self-doubts in the
mind of the man who suddenly found himself occupying the
coach's office of the Washington Redskins.

He had arrived in the nation's capital famed as a man of
offensive genius, coordinator and architect of the record-breaking
passing game of the San Diego Chargers. Locals were weary of
the win-with-defense philosophy of predecessor Jack Pardee, and
they welcomed him with open arms. Joe Gibbs, word had it,
would breathe new life and excitement into the plodding Redskins. Here was a man who would provide the kind of football
team Washington could take pride in.

But things fell apart before Gibbs could even get a good
start. At one point in that 1981 season, there was reason to
believe it would be Washington's worst embarrassment since Wa-
tergate. The Redskins, suffering from every manner of injury
and misfortune imaginable, lost their first five games. This wasn't
winning the soft-spoken, straightforward Gibbs many friends in
his new home. He quickly realized that being a head coach had
demands he had never stopped to consider.

"When I got this job," he says, "I thought to myself, *Okay,
you can finally relax. You're in control of your own destiny at
last.* I knew that whatever happened would come to rest on
my own shoulders, and I was prepared to assume that responsibility. I just assumed I was getting into one of those situations
where, if you were able to do the job, good—if not, it was your
fault.

"What I had never fully comprehended—until we had gone
through that rough early season in '81—was the responsibility
to others that a head coach has. As an individual, you can accept
the defeats because, in most cases, you have a pretty good idea
of why they came about. And your assistants are right in there
with you, seeing the problems you're facing. So, they understand
and so do the players.

"But it doesn't stop there. When things are going bad, you find yourself thinking about the other people you're disappointing. The toughest part of those five straight losses we suffered that year, the thing that was much tougher than I thought it would be, was the disappointment of others so close to the team. I felt a responsibility to the owner, the general manager, and the fans. They had shown a great deal of faith in me, and we were having some pretty rough times. It was a difficult thing for them to have to deal with."

By the time the Redskins had lost their fifth straight game, even Gibbs was beginning to wonder if he would ever realize the satisfaction of his first victory as a head coach. "The more you lose," he says, "the bigger the questions loom. You get down, and if you aren't careful, you get to a point where you expect bad things to happen. You go to work expecting it to be a rotten day."

But before that '81 season became history, the Redskins did an aboutface that caused their annual highlights film to be titled "A Tale of Two Seasons." They finished with eight victories and earned a wildcard place in the playoffs.

The Joe Gibbs success story has enjoyed an upward spiral ever since. A year later, in the strike-shortened season, the Redskins won the Super Bowl with an impressive victory over the Miami Dolphins. A year after that, they returned to the championship game, but there lost to the Los Angeles Raiders.

Though the failure to win a second straight Super Bowl trophy was a disappointment, Redskins followers could salve their feelings with the knowledge that their team had firmly established itself as one of the most legitimate powerhouses in NFL history.

And more than a little credit, they realized, was due Gibbs.

"Joe impresses me now just as he did back when we were first talking to him about the job," says Redskins owner Jack Kent Cooke. "He's an ambitious man with the ability to make that ambition work. As a coach, he's a pioneer, really—a man who recognized before others the perceptible change that was to occur in the character of our game. When people look back years from now, they'll have to recognize Joe as a man who changed the offensive philosophy of pro football."

Joe Gibbs did not finally come to his head coaching job flying by the seat of his pants. Few NFL head coaches have spent as much time on the training grounds as he did.

A tight end and linebacker for coach Don Coryell at San Diego State, Gibbs remained on campus after graduation to serve as line coach. This was before Florida State's Bill Peterson persuaded him to move there as his offensive coordinator. Two years later, Southern California's John McKay was in need of a line coach and placed a call to the young Gibbs. After two seasons with the Trojans, Gibbs moved to the University of Arkansas to coach quarterbacks.

Then, in 1973, he was reunited with Coryell and first introduced to the world of professional football. Working as the offensive backfield coach, Gibbs played a vital role in two NFC east division titles won by the St. Louis Cardinals during his five-year stay. Thereafter, McKay, having moved from Southern California to direct the fortunes of the newly formed Tampa Bay Buccaneers, persuaded Gibbs to join his staff as offensive coordinator.

A year later, however, Coryell was head coach of the San Diego Chargers and rehired his most celebrated student as his offensive coordinator. It was there that Gibbs, who had learned that a road map was an essential tool of the coaching trade, began to gain nationwide recognition. The Chargers, with veteran Dan Fouts as quarterback, revolutionized the passing attack, rewriting NFL records. And with each new season, each new record, Gibbs's stock rose.

But the opportunity to serve as his own boss had not come. Gibbs was weary of the moving and frustrated over being ignored whenever other NFL head jobs came open. So, he began thinking of another course of action.

"I began to think that maybe I should begin pursuing a college head-coaching job," he says. "I felt I was getting a little old to still be an assistant. And I was afraid that I would get to a point where people would think I was too old to move up into a head coaching job. Each year, I thought about it a little more than the one before. It was getting to a point where I was letting it upset me during the off-season."

It was at the end of the 1980 season, however, that Chargers owner Joe Klein called Gibbs into his office and informed him that a couple of teams in the league had expressed interest in interviewing him for head-coaching jobs.

Joe Gibbs made no attempt to hide his excitement. He began to think the long wait was finally over.

You know the rest. Washington general manager Bobby Beathard called to advise him that he was high on the list of candidates for the Redskins job. They met, they talked, and an agreement was reached. Gibbs called his wife, Patricia, and sons, Jason and Coy, to tell them that they would soon have a new address.

The dream was finally going to come true.

In truth, the pursuit of a head-coaching job was not the only struggle Gibbs was facing. As he moved from one job to another, learning and feeling his ambition grow, he was also advancing in another area. A man who had decided early in life that he believed in God, Gibbs was realizing that growth as a Christian was another goal he wished to achieve.

"It's not really difficult to determine your belief," he says. "You simply make a choice. Were we an accident? Or did God create us? I made that decision as a young man. I knew in my heart that I was no accident."

That decision, however, did little to change his priorities. Peer pressures and worldly pleasures beckoned, and Joe Gibbs answered with enthusiasm. "I was after all those things that I had been told would make me happy," he says. "I was grabbing at everything that was available. But every time I did manage to get something I thought I wanted, an empty feeling always seemed to follow. I didn't stop to try to understand it, though. Instead, I just tried for more of whatever it was I thought would bring me happiness."

In 1972, while serving as an assistant at Arkansas, Gibbs learned a lesson that brought the purpose of religion and service of the Lord into proper focus.

There was a gifted young athlete in Pasadena, Texas, whom he had recruited. The youngster was an outstanding quarterback and punter, a gifted basketball player, and a brilliant baseball pitcher. Those who had seen him play were certain that he would one day be pitching in the major leagues. As Gibbs became acquainted with the youngster and his parents, he was impressed by the warmth and love each member of the family felt for each other.

The relationship impressed Gibbs even more when, after several months, he learned that the boy he was recruiting was adopted. "I sensed there was something different in that family's relationship," he says, "but I wasn't sure what it was. Still, I found myself wondering what they had that I didn't. I was more than a little envious."

Eventually, the youngster decided to attend Arkansas and had an outstanding freshman football and baseball season. Then, in his sophomore year, tragedy struck. A serious wrist injury made throwing a football or baseball all but impossible.

"I really felt for that boy," Gibbs recalls. "There he was, nineteen years old and looking ahead to a great athletic career one day, and, the next day, it was all over for him. I was sure the whole world had collapsed on him.

"I called his parents—people I had really come to like a great deal—to see if maybe I could lift their spirits a little. I talked for a while before the boy's mother interrupted me and said, 'Don't worry about Mike. He'll be just fine. He's in God's hands. Whatever happens in his life, we know that he's protected and things will work out as they're supposed to.' I was amazed at how calm and content they seemed to be."

In days to come, he saw the same attitude in the injured young athlete.

"He had such an inner peace," Gibbs recalls. "He had an assurance that came from the knowledge that he was in God's hands. That young man's attitude really got me to thinking."

At the same time, Gibbs was reunited with a coach he had worked with on the staff at Florida State. Gibbs remembered him as a troubled, unhappy man whose life was in constant turmoil. But when this man arrived on the Arkansas campus to join the staff, he was a changed man. He seemed happy, his family relationship, once troubled, was strengthened and fulfilling. The coach had, Gibbs discovered, found Christ.

On a Sunday evening in 1972, Joe Gibbs answered the altar call at the First Baptist Church in Fayetteville, Arkansas. "As I made that walk down the aisle," he says, "I prayed: 'God, I've believed in you in the past, but I haven't been living for you. Help me to show my belief through my actions.' "

Since that evening, Joe Gibbs has given Jesus top priority in his life.

"God doesn't just want us to have a life," he says, "he wants us to have an *abundant* life. That's what he promised. In other words, we should not just be here and live a life, but live a great one. And the only way to achieve this is to have the right relationship with God. As Christians, we're not going through life by ourselves. God has left the Holy Spirit here to provide us with strength and assurance.

"I'm convinced that we all have a purpose and, though it may sound a little crazy, I believe God wanted me to be a football coach. I think that's what he prepared me for and that's why I feel so strongly about what I do."

Such was the attitude Gibbs took with him to Washington. Not only did he take with him his innovative offensive football philosophies, but he also took his faith. When the first pregame chapel service was held after he took over as coach in 1981, there were four in attendance—Gibbs, an assistant coach, and two players. Today, the entire coaching staff, the team, and various other members of the Redskins organization attend regularly.

"Coach Gibbs doesn't force his beliefs on anyone," says All-Pro kicker Mark Moseley. "He's a man who leads by his actions. And he makes his position on things known. His life places God first, then his family, and then football. Those are the three most important things in the lives of anyone in our profession. What you have to be careful about, though, is to not get the priorities out of order. Coach Gibbs has been able to do that, even with all the success he's had and the honors that have come his way. It's a privilege to work for someone like him—someone down to earth. Everything about him is honest."

Defensive end Tony McGee, who has spent fifteen years in the NFL, says, "I've played for a lot of coaches, but never one like Coach Gibbs. He's dedicated his life to the Lord and doesn't mind letting his players know it. He's a man who practices what he believes, and you have to respect that."

Still, Gibbs does very little in the way of overt evangelism. He is quick to point out that he's no preacher. He doesn't intrude on his players' personal lives unless invited. But neither is he one to stand quietly by if he has strong feelings about something regarding his faith.

When an evangelical lobby was called recently in Washington to urge a constitutional amendment on the prayer in public schools issue, Gibbs was on hand, along with fellow coach and Christian Tom Landry of the Dallas Cowboys. "What we as a country need," Gibbs told the session that had been organized by the House Republican Study Committee, "is to put God back in his rightful place in our lives."

This is something that Joe Gibbs, who has now twice been voted the NFL Coach of the Year, has already done. The kids down at the Triangle House can vouch for it.

Andre Thornton

First Baseman, Cleveland Indians

THE CHILLING TEMPERATURES AND oyster-gray skies over the Cleveland area on that October day in 1977 did little to affect the enthusiasm and anticipation of Andre Thornton and his family. The marathon demands of his first year as a member of the Cleveland Indians were successfully behind him, and the off-season held the promise of rest, relaxation, and more time with his family.

For Thornton, first baseman for the Indians, a great season had been written into the history books. It was a marked contrast from life in Chicago where he had spent three frustrating years moving from one position to another. And it was drastically better than in Montreal, where he had labored through most of the 1976 season before being traded again.

In Cleveland, he felt that he had finally found his professional home. Thornton had achieved twenty-eight home runs, seventy runs-batted-in, and a season batting average of .263. It was the latter accomplishment that pleased him most. A year earlier, troubled by the fact that he appeared in just ninety-six games, he had ended the year with only a .194 average and—a ticket out of Canada. Now, however, he was pleased with his progress. As the Indians' cleanup hitter, he was making a contribution, liked the people he was playing with, and felt certain that he would enjoy a long-term relationship with the Cleveland organization.

On that particular Sunday, however, baseball was far from his mind. There would be plenty of time in the weeks to come to regenerate his enthusiasm for the game. For now, he said, he wanted to get far away from it, to rest body and mind.

Andre, his wife, Gertrude, and their children, Andre, Jr., and Theresa, had attended morning church services, enjoyed a quiet afternoon, then returned for evening services. Once back home, Gertrude finished packing while Andre loaded the newly purchased family van for a trip they had been looking forward to for months.

Gertrude's sister was getting married in West Chester, Pennsylvania. The Thorntons planned to stretch their attendance at the ceremonies into a short vacation with her parents. Andre had estimated that the drive would take eight hours; thus, they had decided to travel at night, allowing the children to sleep and also avoiding traffic.

A slight drizzle patted against the windshield as Andre warmed the van, urging everyone to hurry so they might get on their way. Before they backed out of the driveway, his wife offered a brief prayer for a safe journey. She insisted on driving the first few hours, then would turn the wheel over to her husband.

The trip was hardly underway before the drizzle turned to a driving sleet, forcing Gertrude to drive slower than she had planned. The trip was going to take even longer than they had expected. But, the warmth of the van, the soft music playing on the radio, and the bundled children, sleeping comfortably beneath blankets in the back seat, provided the kind of quiet, peaceful atmosphere Andre liked while traveling. Gertrude sensed that her husband was enjoying the drive and said little, dividing her time between the road and occasional mention of the wedding plans.

Andre was napping peacefully by the time the van crossed the Ohio border into Pennsylvania. But as the highway climbed into the mountains, he awoke to a sudden awareness of the hazardous road conditions and turned off the radio to listen to the CB. The sleet was beginning to freeze on the roads ahead as the unexpected storm dramatically worsened. With at least four hours of driving time remaining, he was no longer relaxed.

Just before they arrived at the entrance to the Pennsylvania Turnpike, Andre suggested that his wife pull over and let him take over the driving. Slowly moving back into the now creeping traffic, his full attention was focused on his driving. He approached the task in much the same manner in which he concentrated on pitches thrown to him at bat. It was no time to take risks.

While they were stopped, three-year-old Theresa awoke and sleepily asked if they had arrived at her grandmother's house. Gertrude smiled, told her it would be a while longer, and asked if she would like to move up front to sit in her lap. Theresa eagerly climbed over the seat into her mother's waiting arms and was soon asleep again.

As the van climbed higher into the mountains, Andre reduced his speed to forty miles per hour, then to thirty-five. In addition to the slick roads and the sleet which the windshield wipers were battling against, the wind was funneling through the mountain passes and began to buffet the van. Andre began to think about pulling off the road and waiting for the storm to pass.

Even as he contemplated a stop, however, a blast of wind seemed to lift the back wheels of the van off the road. They were slipping toward the guardrail, skidding sideways across the highway. Desperately, Andre fought to straighten the van, but to no avail.

Gertrude, seeing the guardrail suddenly appear in the near blinding sleet, screamed. It was the last thing Andre Thornton recalled for several minutes.

The next thing he remembered was being on his feet, stumbling through the darkened cold. Through the fog and sleet, he could see cars parked nearby. Atop each was a flashing blue light that struck terror within him. There were voices, but he could not make out what was being said.

Then it suddenly registered on Andre what had happened. He turned to see that the van had completely flipped and was resting on its crumbled roof. Though still dazed, he ran toward the wreckage, screaming at the top of his voice. "Dear Jesus," he said, "please help me. Please, I've got to get my wife and kids out of there."

Even as he spoke a firm hand was on his shoulder. "Take it easy, fella. We're going to get them out for you. Just relax. You need to get to the hospital."

"Where is my family? Are they okay?" The last question was barely audible as Andre's 6'2", 205-pound frame sank to the frozen ground. He had blacked out.

When he came to, he was in a brightly lit emergency room. A nurse stood near him, bandaging a cut on his forehead and telling him that he was going to be all right. Nearby, his five-year-old son, resting on another table, called for him: "Daddy," he said in a faint voice that sent a chill through his father.

"Where's my wife?" Andre asked the nurse. "Where's Theresa? Are they okay?" Already tears were welling in his eyes.

"I'm sorry, Mr. Thornton," the distraught nurse said, "but your wife and daughter didn't survive the accident."

For the next few days, Andre Thornton functioned with a numbness he had never experienced. An avalanche of grief had fallen over him, making the most simple of tasks a monumental chore. Yet he had his son to think about. Somehow, he had to summon the strength and courage to help make him understand the tragedy that had taken his mother and little sister from him. The overwhelming sadness Andre saw in the piercing dark eyes of his son was heartbreaking. Yet he tried his best to explain the loss to him and offer whatever comfort he could.

A minister arrived and stayed with Thornton and his son. Tearfully, they prayed together, giving thanks for the good times Andre had shared with his wife and daughter and asking God to welcome them into his kingdom. Andre, a devout Christian, also prayed for strength to deal with the tragedy.

In West Chester, the wedding was canceled, and the anticipated good cheer was replaced by the somber task of funeral preparations. Andre and his son were released from the hospital and driven to their final destination by the minister who had stayed with them in the hospital.

"As we made that trip," Thornton recalls, "I felt that life had been ripped right out of me. But, at the same time, I felt a peace that could only come from God. Gert and I had married young—she was nineteen and I was twenty—and we grew up together knowing the Lord. We spent seven years together, blessed by him. I knew that the same God who had so blessed us through those years was the one who would be there to take me through the hurt and sorrow I had to deal with."

And it was Andre who showed the greatest strength in those days immediately following the accident. Upon arriving in West Chester, he was approached by one of his wife's cousins, a woman with whom both he and Gertrude had unsuccessfully tried to share their faith on numerous occasions. "You've told me of a loving, caring God," she said, anger mixed with her tears. "How could he do this? Is this the way he repays the commitment you and Gert had?"

Andre cradled her in his arms and told her that he didn't fully understand what had happened and that he was devastated by the loss. "But," he added, "all I know is that God does things for a reason. I've got to trust him. He's all I've got to hang on to."

The funeral was attended by several of Thornton's teammates. Second baseman Duane Kuiper was there, as was former Indian third baseman Buddy Bell, and manager Jeff Torborg.

Andre sat silently with his son as the minister completed the services, then rose and asked that he be allowed to speak. Turning to those in attendance, he stood with tears streaming down his face and said, "Before another life slips away—perhaps a loved one of yours—I pray that you will know God as I do, for only he can help you in a time like this."

Torborg sat, watching Andre as the procession filed out

of the church. "I've never experienced anything so moving in all my life," he says. "There Andre stood, as torn up as any man I've ever seen, with his young son beside him, trying to offer comfort to the rest of us in the congregation. I had known that he was a remarkable man, but not really just how remarkable until that moment.

"It was a month later, at Thanksgiving, when I called him, just to see if he was getting along okay and to ask if there was anything I might do to help. We talked for quite some time and, before our conversation ended, he had helped me with some personal problems I was having. The inner strength of the man is incredible."

This had not always been the case.

Born in Tuskegee, Alabama, Andre Thornton grew up in Phoenixville, Pennsylvania, near Philadelphia. He spent much of his boyhood angry, frustrated, and anxious to strike out at his adversaries. Athletics offered him a way to take on some of those enemies.

A football player as well as a baseball standout in high school, Andre admits that he played the game on the razor's edge of the rules. "I was a blocking back," he says, "and a pretty good one. After I'd knock someone down, I'd step on him to make sure he wasn't going to get up too quickly. I wanted to hurt people. Back then, my rule of thumb was to get to them before they got to me."

It was a philosophy without joy. Maybe he was a good football player, but it earned him no real friendships, no really warm sense of accomplishment. So what if he could run eighty balls on the pool table, picking up pretty good spending money with his hustling? It didn't bring him the kind of lasting satisfaction he was seeking. The prejudice, the violence, and the day-to-day human misery that formed the backdrop of his adolescence made Andre a bitter person even before he was a man.

One of his older brothers died when Andre was very young; a close friend was drowned; another was stabbed. Buddies went off to Vietnam and returned broken or maimed, if they came back at all.

Even Andre's home life made no sense to him. His father was an alcoholic, leaving the raising of seven children to his mother. "Looking back," Andre says, "I have to believe that the only thing that kept my mother going at times was her tremendous faith in God."

It was, in fact, a small gift from his mother that finally brought order to Andre's life. He was eighteen years old and attending a National Guard camp when he suddenly felt more alone, more insignificant than he had at any time in his life. "It just kind of swept over me," he remembers. "There I was, eighteen, in good health, and had just signed a major league baseball contract with the Philadelphia Phillies. I had everything in the world to look forward to. But suddenly I felt totally disillusioned and very alone."

He turned to a religious tract his mother had given him and began to read it nightly. Soon, he was reading the Bible as well. "That tract my mother gave me was the first step toward my understanding my purpose in life. I began to understand why every joy I had ever experienced had been so short-lived. Hitting a home run or winning a game just wasn't enough; it wasn't lasting. The two questions I had worried over most of my life were: Why are we here? What happens to us after we die? Those questions became easier to answer after I realized that Christ had a purpose for me. I realized that if I was going to feel the kind of peace and satisfaction I so badly wanted, it could only be accomplished by serving God and living in accordance with his will."

That realization helped him through many rough spots in the early days of his professional career. "I didn't exactly tear up the league when I first got here," he grins. "Then, when Chicago traded me to Montreal, I had some serious doubts whether I'd make it as a professional ball player. Being sent to Montreal was like being exiled to the desert. I had to ask the Lord if that was what he really had in mind for me. Frankly, I was hoping he had made a mistake. But I knew deep down that wasn't the case. I went up there and had a terrible year. I was injured and wasn't hitting the ball well at all. I was at the bottom of my career.

"But as a Christian, I was able to grow, to make something positive from the adversity I was dealing with. The experience in Montreal, in retrospect, allowed me to greatly improve my witness for the Lord."

Then came the trade to the Indians and the good 1977 season. Andre was happy, Gertrude was happy, and the future seemed to promise smooth sailing—until that tragic night of October 17.

Many of Andre's friends and teammates silently wondered if he would ever recover from his terrible loss. A sensitive and loving man, he had given his family a far greater priority than his athletic career. Some feared that he was likely to withdraw from the public life of baseball and dwell privately on his overwhelming sorrow. There were many willing to wager that Andre Thornton would not be around for the 1978 major league season.

Obviously, no one realized his strength.

"As a Christian," he says, "I knew there would be a lot of people watching me, waiting to see how I responded. They knew of my faith and were waiting to see how I would respond to its being tested so. And I knew there were those waiting to see if I would fall on my face. During those dark days after the accident, I spent a lot of time in prayer, asking for strength to go on.

"The thing that made it possible to get through it all was the knowledge that I wasn't alone. I had a lot of friends and family eager to lend support. And I was always keenly aware of God's presence. I sought his help and it was given."

When spring training began, he was back in uniform, anxious and eager. There was no sign of bitterness or anger. What resulted was the best season he had ever enjoyed as a major leaguer. He hit five more home runs than he had hit the previous season, and his RBI totals increased by thirty-five.

It was after an early season game in which he'd driven in two runs that one of his teammates approached him in the postgame locker room to offer congratulations. "Look, Andre," he said, "I don't really know how to put this, but I've got to ask you something. After what happened to your family, how are you able to do it? You're so positive, so full of life. I think it's wonderful, but, frankly, I don't understand it. If I had experienced what you've been through, I would have gone crazy."

Thornton smiled and explained to his teammate how God had given him strength to go on. Before the conversation ended,

Andre had persuaded his teammate to attend the team's next Sunday morning baseball chapel.

"I wasn't at all surprised that Andre came back and had the kind of season he did in 1978," says friend and teammate Kuiper. "In fact, nothing surprises me about the guy. Not only is he a powerful man but he's genuine. He's no hypocrite just running off at the mouth. Years from now, if someone asks me who I remember most from baseball, it will be Andre Thornton— not just because of his religious beliefs, but because of the kind of person he is."

The career of thirty-four-year-old Andre Thornton has not been without its ups and downs since that remarkable return to the game in '78, however. A right knee that required two operations, a broken right hand, and a broken thumb forced him to miss all of the 1980 season and most of 1981. But in '82, he returned, enthusiastic as ever, and played well enough to win the American League Comeback Player of the Year award.

Since then, he has performed well as the Indians' designated hitter, utilizing his strength and power to continue driving in runs and hitting homers.

And he's married to the daughter of a minister who is also a gospel singer. Together, Gail and Andre Thornton are active in a variety of Christian activities in the Cleveland area. Andre currently serves as president of the Christian Family Outreach and is a member of the board of the Professional Athletes Outreach. Regularly, they witness together. Andre speaks, often telling audiences of the accident that so tested his faith; Gail sings.

"We're very happy," Andre says. "I look at it this way: Gertrude and I had seven wonderful years together; and I know that one day I will see her and my daughter again in heaven. If I didn't believe that, I couldn't go on living. At the same time, Andre, Jr., and I now have another wonderful person in our lives, and it means a great deal to both of us.

"It's as if I've lived two lives, really. There are times now when the past with Gert and Theresa seems like a dream. I no longer feel the sense of loss I once did. Now, I'm just grateful that I've found two women like Gert and Gail in one lifetime.

"I know now that Gert's death was a part of God's plan.

Her death has been given purpose by the hundreds of people who have come to know Christ because of her."

All of Andre Thornton's victories, then, have not come on the playing field. There are triumphs, far removed from athletics, that he treasures.

Several months after the funeral of Gertrude and Theresa he received a call from the cousin who had expressed such anger that God had allowed such a tragedy.

"Andre," she said, "I've accepted Christ as my personal Savior. I wanted you to be the first to know. Gert told me that there would come a time when I would feel the need to have Christ in my life, but I never believed her. It didn't make any sense to me—until she died.

"At the funeral, when everyone was so broken up, you seemed so calm, so at peace. I knew how much you loved Gert and, quite honestly, I couldn't understand why you seemed to handle it so much better than the rest of us. But the more I thought about it, the more I realized I wanted that same peace you seemed to have. Thank you for showing me the way."

That moment, Andre says, was more rewarding than any home run he's ever hit.

Bob Breunig

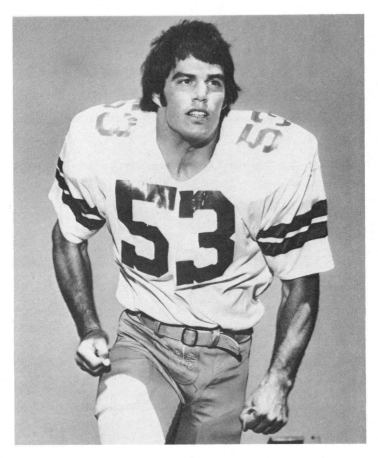

Former Linebacker, Dallas Cowboys

BOB BREUNIG, WHO HAD LABORED as the starting line-backer for the Dallas Cowboys through most of his ten-year professional career, sat outside the team's dressing room and watched a thunderstorm building in the distance. In a sense, the storm provided an appropriate backdrop, a proper accent for the frustrating times he was enduring.

43

The 1984 season had been one of storm clouds and confusion, injury and upheaval for Breunig, the three-time pro-bowl selection. Sometime in the distant future, he probably will look back on it as the year he became the media's "whipping boy."

The ever-winning Dallas Cowboys were stumbling and struggling to gain a spot in the playoffs for the tenth straight year, and fault-finders were having a field day. A season-long quarterback controversy had split the team into two highly vocal factions. There were those who had given up on veteran Danny White and insisted that backup Gary Hogeboom was the man for the job. Others warned of Hogeboom's inexperience and argued for White.

Elsewhere, there was the feeling that Dallas's problems could not be solved simply by switching quarterbacks. The truth of the matter seemed to be that the Cowboys, who had appeared in five Super Bowls—winning two of them—were not the team of old. Too many bad player drafts, too many retirements, and too much dissension had reduced them to something less than championship contenders.

Thus, as the franchise celebrated its twenty-fifth year in the league with a nine-to-seven record and no appearance in the playoffs, the team was fair game for the critics. From coast-to-coast, it seemed that it was open season on "America's team." And Bob Breunig was not exempt from the raging criticism.

From the time the up-and-down campaign got underway, he had been the focal point of unusual attention—and the target of painfully negative comments. The media and fans suggested that Breunig, once one of the most vital forces in the Dallas defense, had become a liability. If the opposition succeeded in breaking a play up the middle, fingers immediately pointed at Breunig. The "Monday morning quarterbacks" counted his Sunday tackles like picking so many nits. They were saying that Breunig had lost that all-important step—maybe even his enthusiasm for the game.

Through it all, however, Breunig remained quiet, refusing to seek out a soapbox from which to defend himself.

Looking back on the troubled season, linebacker coach Jerry Tubbs shook his head. "There is a great deal of unfairness in this game," he said. "Everyone deserves criticism because, at times, everyone is going to be at fault. But so much of what was dealt Bob was not justified. Take our game against New

Orleans, for instance. They broke a long run up the middle and immediately everyone was blaming Bob. It wasn't his fault at all.

"I'm not saying he had a year like he's had in the past, but he didn't grade badly at all. Certainly, he didn't play as badly as some people seemed to believe. It's one thing to get blamed for things that are your fault. But when people start finding fault, they tend to begin seeing things that aren't really there. That's where the unfairness takes over.

"But Bob handled all the criticism and bad press very well. In fact, I don't know how anyone could have handled it any better. He just kept working, practicing when probably he shouldn't have, getting himself ready to do as good a job as he could do."

It wasn't easy. Late in the summer prior to the '84 season, concern developed over a nagging neck injury Breunig had suffered with for several years. Only after a specialist assured him there were no serious problems did he decide to make the annual trek to Thousand Oaks, California, for training camp. Once there, however, he reinjured his neck in the first week of practice. Valuable practice time was lost as he was forced to stand on the sidelines, awaiting the doctor's okay to go back to work.

Then, once that problem disappeared, he injured his back during a routine practice drill. The back problem eventually triggered all the criticism. On several occasions during the season, Breunig spent mid-week time in the hospital in traction to relieve the pain so that he might be able to play on Sunday. He once had to miss a practice because the back spasms suddenly returned as he bent over to lace up his shoes. Yet he was in the lineup two days later. He even had a hospital bed, complete with traction equipment, moved into his home in an attempt to correct the problem.

What resulted from the soreness and pain was a year in which he was never 100 percent healthy. The time came when he heard a chorus of boos from the stands in Texas Stadium as he was introduced as the starting middle linebacker. Finally, when the pain grew so intense that he was unable to practice, he went to head coach Tom Landry and spoke the words he had never thought he would say. He suggested that rookie Eugene Lockhart take his place.

Breunig then resigned himself to spending the remainder

of the year on the injured reserve list, watching the games in street clothes, and offering suggestions and advice to the youngster who had taken over his job.

"The whole thing was very frustrating," Breunig admits, "not being able to play up to my capabilities and then finally not being able to play at all. But it was something I couldn't really control. So I tried as best as I could to put it out of my mind."

Patience and a strong Christian faith helped, as did the example set by friend and teammate Danny White, who had quietly absorbed the criticisms and fan taunts during the afore-mentioned quarterback dilemma.

"I learned a lot from Danny," Breunig says. "Throughout the difficult times he was dealing with, he maintained a very positive attitude. He managed to keep his priorities in order. In fact, he told me at one point that the whole matter of being benched [while Hogeboom directed the Cowboys' number one unit for much of the first half of the season] helped him to realize that football wasn't as important as a lot of other things in his life.

"I think we all tend to lose our perspective at times. To a lot of people, how many tackles I make on Sunday afternoons is a very important thing. And it is important; don't get me wrong. But it isn't the end-all, believe me. In fact, if you started trying to write a list of priorities on paper, your arm would be worn out before you got to one about Bob Breunig's performance in a particular football game.

"I have a friend, for instance, who is in his early thirties and has cancer. Another friend of mine has a new baby who was born with spina bifida and is in the hospital. I visit kids and elderly people in hospitals a great deal—people who have far greater problems than I do.

"Now, how do you even begin to relate how I perform in a football game to things like that?"

A Christian since his senior year at Arizona State, Bob Breunig is one of those gifted athletes who loves the game he plays but does view it as something less than the alpha and omega of his existence. It is a stance that has drawn both applause and criticism. There are those, frankly, who have great difficulty embracing the idea that a Christian can be properly aggressive once the game whistle blows.

One Dallas writer, in fact, went so far as to suggest that "if Breunig would put his Bible away and think more about knocking someone into the nickel seats, he might be a better football player."

Once again, Tubbs—himself a former middle linebacker for the Cowboys—comes to his pupil's defense. "People only have to look at what Bob's done during his career to realize he's one of the most dedicated football players ever to wear a Dallas uniform. He works hard every time he steps on the practice field; and on game day, you can rest assured he's going to give you everything he has. I've never seen Bob hold back an ounce. The guy's a winner, pure and simple. That's why he's been around as long as he has. That's why he's been to the Pro Bowl several times and wears a Super Bowl ring.

"He's an outstanding competitor whom I admire a great deal. At the same time, I have even greater admiration for Bob as a Christian. The attitude he has about life, about other people, is a model for all of us. There have been a lot of lives affected in a very positive way just because of an association with Bob Breunig."

"I've been aware of the criticisms for a long time," Breunig says, "but I've always believed a Christian stands on firm ground, so I'm not intimidated by what others think. Frankly, I had some difficulties at first in balancing the violence of football with my beliefs. Then I realized that we aren't asked to be stereotype Christians. God wants us to be complete persons. There's a time to be intense and competitive and excited. The key is, what's the intent in your heart? Are you out on the field to play the game fairly, or to try and hurt somebody? I think I've been a better football player because God mandates a disciplined life. That knowledge charges me up. I'm convinced that God wants me to be a football player. And that he feels whatever you do you should do with all your heart and soul."

There is, Tubbs points out, a long-perpetuated myth that the Cowboys' famed "flex defense" is designed to direct all running plays in the direction of the middle linebacker. If it works properly, virtually every tackle should be made by Breunig.

"We sat down the other day," says All-Pro defensive tackle

Randy White, "and tried to figure out just how many of our defensive alignments were actually designed to free Bob to make the tackle. We finally came up with two or three. If he just stood there in the middle on every play, he'd be out of position 90 percent of the time."

Breunig has spent most of his career battling against another myth. Somewhere in the clichés of sports, it has been determined that anyone playing middle linebacker in the NFL should dedicate himself to spending his athletic life just one step from felony indictment. To him, the rules are made to be broken. He should, to continue the jargon, be something of a wild man, neither shy about poking fingers in highly paid halfbacks' eyes or biting them on the leg—sometimes after the play has been whistled dead by the officials. They dress it up a little in the press releases, calling said performers "aggressive."

Then, there is Dallas's Bob Breunig. A guy who seems always to be smiling, he has recorded songs of a Christian bent for children, and delivers warmly and articulately on a daily radio show. And he actually enjoys helping his wife, Mary, sell a cookbook whose earnings go to aid children at the Happy Hill Farm Children's Home in Glen Rose, Texas. He's active in the Fellowship of Christian Athletes, the Professional Athletes Outreach, and is president of the Sixty-five Roses Club which benefits the Cystic Fibrosis Foundation. His home is the site for a weekly Bible study, attended by as many as twenty teammates and friends each Thursday evening.

He has spent a superlative athletic career in violation of the image many pro linebackers work hard to maintain. Bob Breunig marches to a different drummer—but not, as his credentials prove, without success in large measures.

As a collegian, he was an All-American selection, then came to the Cowboys as a third-round draft pick in 1975. He was, the coaching staff agreed, ideally suited to handle the job of middle linebacker in Dallas's complicated defense. He wasn't likely to break many bones, but neither would he make many mistakes.

He is, by his own definition, a thinking man's linebacker. "I work hard at my job. I do everything possible to be the best I can be, and I think I approach the game with a very high level of intensity," he says. Then, almost as an afterthought, he adds another ingredient.

"I'm also aggressive. At least as aggressive as I can be within the framework of our defense. I force things. I go after the football. I like to make the tackle. But, no, I don't think I could ever be one of those who goes out to see just how badly I can rough someone up. That, to me, isn't the purpose or the intent of the game. I play within the rules and within the restrictions of our kind of defensive scheme."

Could, then, Jack Lambert of the Pittsburgh Steelers—a free-wheeling, head-knocking type middle linebacker—enjoy success in the Cowboys' system? "Oh, sure," says Breunig, "he could play 'the flex.' He'd just have to contain himself more, be a little more restrictive in his movements and a little more patient."

The second part of the question is not even asked before the answer is offered: "And yes, I believe I could play the position in an open style of defense if I had to."

For Breunig, however, "the flex" approach is ideally suited to his personality and his philosophy. While he shies away from the goody-goody image some have hung on him, he is a strong believer in Christian values. And he's going to play the game fairly even if it causes him to be labeled something less than a swing-from-the-floor type of defender.

This is not to say that he marches to the straightest of lines dictated by "the flex" philosophy.

"There are times," he admits, "when I'll wing it a little. But that chance taking comes with maturity and experience and knowledge of the system. I'm one of those who firmly believes the best way to do things is by the book most of the time. But there are occasions when you do have some options, and once you're comfortable with your abilities, you can maneuver some within the framework of the system.

"What it all boils down to is something Coach [Tom] Landry is constantly pointing out to us in meetings: A pro makes the play."

Throughout his career, Bob Breunig has done just that— until the bothersome back injury forced him to the sidelines late in the '84 season.

"As a Christian," he says, "I know the Lord allows each of us a certain amount of adversity. Through this you build character. I know I grew some during the whole experience and probably have a much better perspective on things because of the injury and the criticism and all.

"In truth, I have no gripes coming. I've had a great number of wonderful things happen to me as a result of my association with the Dallas Cowboys. My cup runneth over. There's not a computer big enough to record the good things that have happened to me and my family."

There are those who will say that such statements are generally voiced by those contemplating retirement from the game. "Anyone who has been in the league ten years and has had some injury problems has to be thinking about when he might hang it up," Breunig said just before announcing his retirement in January 1985. "For now, though, I'm taking it one day at a time."

Meanwhile, he had already begun grooming his own replacement. When injury forced him out of the lineup, the job went to a promising rookie, Eugene Lockhart. Breunig spent a great deal of time with him, discussing the philosophy of the Cowboys' defense, making suggestions, and offering encouragement.

"It's a pleasure to work with a guy like Lockhart," Breunig says. "He's one of those who stays after meetings, is the first in line for drills, remains after practice, and asks questions. He's also got a very positive attitude."

Lockhart sounds much like another Bob Breunig. And if that is the case, the Cowboys' middle linebacking job is in good hands.

A few drops of rain began to fall. The storm had arrived. Because of his back problems, Breunig had no workout to look forward to. And so he continued with his reflections.

"You know, toward the end of my senior year at Arizona State, I had a wonderful experience. I had come to a point where I was looking for more than what was obvious in life. I knew I was going to have a professional football contract, I had friends and family. But it didn't all add up to what I wanted. I realized every satisfaction I was enjoying was just temporary.

"I had some good friends, an older couple in Los Angeles, who had just become Christians, and they helped me a great deal. They began pointing me in a direction that would lead me to the kind of everlasting satisfaction I was searching for. So did a professor who taught a course on 'Biblical Backgrounds for Literature.' As I studied, facts became clearer, and I began to change inside."

He also began to read the Bible regularly.

"There's more to life than day-to-day living," he says. "A man has to be balanced. The Bible is a practical handbook for living. It covers all your relationships—with your wife, your children, your peers, your superiors, your opponents. And it tells the story of the greatest person who ever lived. You can't begin to be Christlike without knowing about Jesus. I've never been one to believe that reading the Bible makes you any more successful—but it does help you deal with life."

And this is something that Bob Breunig, despite injury and criticism, does very well.

Glenn and Lyle Blackwood

The "Bruise Brothers," Miami Dolphins

THOUGH THE SUPER BOWL was but a matter of days away and pressure was building, Glenn and Lyle Blackwood—the Texas-born brothers who work together in the Miami Dolphins secondary—were relaxed, laughing and swapping stories. One would have thought the rewards and fame attached to participating in the National Football League championship were of no real concern.

"Listen," says Glenn, reflecting back on boyhood days in San Antonio, "he's my brother and all, and I personally like the guy. But the fact of the matter is, he's nuts—and always has been. I remember once, when I was just a little kid, I built this fort out of dried Christmas trees I collected around the neighborhood. Lyle even offered to help me, which was pretty unusual. Once we got it built, I crawled inside to check it out. As soon as I did, Lyle set fire to it."

Lyle laughs and offers his own version, "It wasn't a big fire. Shoot, I just set fire to the entrance. He had plenty of time to get out."

"I'm lucky to be here," Glenn says with mock seriousness.

Such is the byplay constantly carried on by the brother combination that has helped the Dolphins to become one of the best teams in the NFL. Off the field, the Blackwoods are fun-loving and relaxed. When the whistle blows, they do their best to live up to the nickname given them several years ago by a Miami sportswriter—the Bruise Brothers.

They stand, then, as positive proof that committed Christians need not be passive.

"I don't know that I've ever been around two players who approach the game with any more intensity and dedication," says veteran Miami head coach Don Shula. "Each is a very aggressive kind of player, and neither likes to lose. They don't go out on Sunday afternoon with the idea of hurting anybody; but, when they make a tackle, the other guy's likely to remember it for a while. That's their style.

"By the same token, you're going to have to look a long time before you can find anyone who doesn't have the highest respect for the way they play the game. They play it by the rules. And when the game's over, they're going to be across the field shaking hands with the other fellas.

"Lyle and Glenn are the best examples I know of what Christians are supposed to be. They work hard to be the best they can be at what they do with the abilities the Lord has dealt them. And, when work time is over, they know how to enjoy life—being around people and making others enjoy being around them. If you're down about something, the best remedy

I know is to get around the Blackwoods for a little while. It doesn't take them long to put a smile on your face. I don't think I've ever been around people more at peace with themselves.

"Now, I'm not sure what theologians might tell you, but the things I've just mentioned are what being a Christian is all about, at least to me. Lyle and Glenn pass all the tests with flying colors."

But this hasn't always been the case. Time was when one of the brothers ran on a course pockmarked with self-destruction. For a while, the other wasn't that far behind. Long before Lyle and Glenn Blackwood were donating time and energy to the Fellowship of Christian Athletes, Youth for Christ, and Campus Crusade for Christ, they were drawn to life's faster lanes where neon lit the way.

Lyle, the elder at age thirty-three, can look back at a walk on the wild side, which at one time threatened not only the career he so badly wanted but his health as well.

As a teenager, he gave sports precedence over academics. The only reason for any attention to studies, he admits, was the rule that required passing grades to be eligible for football in the fall, basketball in the winter, and baseball in the spring. Though he stood only 5'9" and weighed no more than 145 pounds, Lyle was regarded as one of the premier athletes at San Antonio's Winston Churchill High School. But, while peers and opponents were impressed with his talents, college coaches—the men who handed out the much-desired athletic scholarships—spent little time seeking Lyle Blackwood's home address.

"If you're a good football player in a Texas high school," Lyle points out, "you dream of getting a scholarship offer to play for one of the teams in the Southwest Conference. Every year I would look up to the guys who were seniors, getting offers to play at the University of Texas or Baylor or wherever. That really impressed me. I knew that was what I wanted more than anything, and I couldn't wait until I was a senior.

"An athletic scholarship is a financial blessing to the family, of course, but I never really considered that aspect. I looked at it as a kind of award. If you didn't get a scholarship, it was like a public announcement that you really weren't all that hot."

Ultimately, that announcement was made about Lyle Black-

wood. Because of his size, no major college scouts came calling
and begging for his services. Embarrassed and angry, he first
considered junking the idea of even going to college. Then, he
made up his mind to prove those who had ignored him wrong.
Enrolled in Blinn Junior College, he spent two years playing in
its defensive secondary, intercepting a school record of fifteen
passes. And he began to grow, slowly at first, then in welcomed
leaps. After his second season of junior college football, Lyle
was just over six-feet tall and had added forty pounds to his
muscular frame.

At the time, the coaches at Texas Christian University were
searching the junior college marketplace for immediate help for
their sagging football program. They had followed Lyle's two-
year progress, liked what they saw, and offered him a scholarship.

It was a different Lyle Blackwood who enrolled at TCU
in 1971. No longer the introverted youngster, too small for big-
time athletics, he arrived in Fort Worth with a confident manner
that bordered on cockiness. He was at last in the big time and
made plans to enjoy every minute of it. Indeed, in the next two
years, he was honored on the All-Southwest Conference team
despite the fact that TCU's seasons continued to be dismal. By
the time he was a senior, he had already begun to contemplate
his next athletic step. Several pro scouts had been in touch with
him, telling him they were certain he would be a relatively high
draft choice. Next stop—the NFL.

In the 1973 draft, Lyle was selected in the ninth round
by the Denver Broncos. That 217 college players had been picked
ahead of him didn't affect his confidence in the slightest. He
was certain Denver had big plans for him; they had told him
so. There had been a handsome bonus that went with his signing
a $21,000 contract. "I figured I was set for life," he recalls. "There
I was, just out of college and making more money than my
dad. I was pretty impressed with myself."

Unfortunately, officials of the Broncos didn't share Lyle's
feelings. Before the regular season had opened, he was given
his release. "We made a real mistake with him," Denver front
office executive Carroll Hardy said. Lyle Blackwood's athletic
career was back to square one. All the obstacles he had overcome—his size, the rebuff by college scouts—seemed for naught,

and a depression unlike any he'd ever experienced set in.

He was claimed on waivers by the Cincinnati Bengals and earned a place on the team as a punt returner and a backup defensive back. Never happy with his situation, Lyle worked harder at being a man-about-town than he did at being a professional football player. Even more introverted than he had been as a schoolboy, he turned to a drink-and-drug lifestyle. When mellowed by booze or high on drugs, he reasoned, he became more personable, more outgoing. If he couldn't fit into the pro-football world, he decided that he could find a way to fit into the fun-loving social world that existed on the perimeter of big-time athletics.

"I felt that to be normal," he says, "I had to do the things that would help me fit into the crowd." And, while he stops short of any vivid descriptions of the depths to which the drug and alcohol problems took him, he does make a telling point: "The first thing alcohol and drugs do is numb the moral portion of the brain."

He found himself in a position of running everywhere and getting nowhere. Cincinnati teammate Bob Trumpy, who had a locker near Lyle in the Bengals' training room, recalls those days when his teammate was living the fast-lane life. "I don't know how he did it. When he came to the practice field in the mornings, you could have drawn blood from his eyes. He was burning the candle at both ends as fast as a man could. A lot of people tried to talk to him, to explain that he was damaging his chances of ever really establishing himself on the team, not to mention his health. But Lyle just didn't have time to listen to anybody but his own drummer. The guy put his body through so much abuse during the week that everyone wondered how he was able to play on Sundays. In the end, it cost him his job."

After three years of frustration, Blackwood went to general manager Mike Brown and told him he didn't feel he'd been treated fairly and asked to be traded. The Bengals were quick to grant his request. When the 1976 season opened, he was the property of the Seattle Seahawks.

Still clinging to the fast lane, Lyle's one-year tenure in Seattle was less than memorable. He was injured for much of the season. When training camp opened the following summer, head coach Jack Patera called Blackwood into his office and told him that he was again being placed on waivers.

Though he was wondering if his lot in life was to be that of a journeyman pro-ball player, Blackwood took something positive away from his brief tenure in Seattle.

"While I was with the Seahawks," he says, "I roomed with [quarterback] Jim Zorn. Though he wasn't one to preach to others, he was very firm in his Christian beliefs. I've never known anyone who was more at peace and content with his life.

"He realized I had problems but he waited for me to bring them up. When we were on the road, I would go out and get drunk, running crazy on the streets. Then I'd come back to find him in bed, maybe watching television, getting himself mentally ready for the game the next day. I have to believe I offended him a great deal with my actions, but he was very patient with me.

"And there were other guys on the team—Norm Evans and Jim Largent—who had the kind of peace of mind and sense of purpose that being a Christian gives you. I envied them and wondered how they had managed to get where they were in their lives. I talked with them a little about it and realized they were eager to help. At the same time, they shot straight with me—the only person who could really get Lyle Blackwood on the right road was Lyle Blackwood."

By then married to his wife, Suzanne, Lyle knew a dramatic change was in order if the marriage was to survive. "I'm not saying that things changed overnight," he says, "but I did begin to take a hard look at my priorities. Football was still very important to me. I badly wanted to prove I could play regularly in the NFL. But above all, I wanted to be a good person, a good husband, a good father, and a good friend to others.

"I'd spent too much time trying to make myself happy and had failed pretty miserably. I was miserable. I began to realize how really immature I was. I had money and a little status. Even though I wasn't making much of an impact as a player, I was, after all, still in the NFL. And I thought that somehow put me above everything. I didn't spend much time looking beyond the end of my own nose. I lived my life one day at a time, thinking all the while it would never end. I rationalized that the guys who had released me wouldn't know a talented football player if they saw one."

The next stop on Lyle's football odyssey was Baltimore.

There, he finally began to emerge as a bonafide NFL player, earning a starting position with the Colts and leading the league in interceptions with ten in 1977. He had reached a new high in his athletic career, but the much-desired transition of his personal life was a far greater struggle. By his own admission, his marriage was miserable. And, once removed from the Sunday afternoon adrenalin flow of the games, so was his life.

Still, he wore the facade of the happy-go-lucky jock. Once he was chased from the Colts dressing room by All-Pro tackle George Kunz. "George was a real doughnut freak," Lyle recalls. "So, for several days, I left a couple for him in his locker. Then, one day, I dipped a couple of them in wax beforehand. They just looked like regular glazed doughnuts. George had already finished one by the time he realized what I'd done. I think if he'd caught me that day my career would have ended right there."

But overshadowing the practical joking was a lingering frustration that the personal changes he had attempted to make didn't seem to be working. He became increasingly defensive and angry. At the end of his third season with the Colts, he again asked to be traded. Maybe, he thought, a change of scenery, a new environment, might provide him with a better attitude.

"I was still kidding myself," he says. "I was not ready to take responsibility for my own actions."

At age thirty, Lyle reported to the preseason training camp of the New York Giants in the summer of 1981. Weary of the trials and battles to earn a spot for himself on yet another roster, he did little more than go through the motions. "I tried to get into it emotionally, but just couldn't seem to. I think the Giants had about the same attitude toward me. They cut me before the season got underway.

"I knew that physically I could still play, and deep down I knew I wanted to; but for some reason, I just couldn't generate the kind of enthusiasm I knew was necessary. After the Giants released me, I got a call from Detroit, offering me a tryout. I had gone from being a fairly high draft choice to one of the hundreds of guys who just walks in with a million-to-one shot at making it in pro ball. After the tryout, though, I was pretty confident the Lions were going to sign me. But they didn't. I decided it was time to begin looking a little harder at the real world."

Moving to Austin, he took over the management of a fried chicken restaurant. Without the complications of pro football, he told friends, his life was getting better. Things at home were settling down, the drinking and drugs were a thing of the past. He was enjoying the stability of what he liked to refer to as a "normal" life, and he was working harder than ever at becoming a Christian.

Still, on Sunday afternoons, he watched the NFL games on TV, just in case a member of someone's defensive backfield went down with an injury. Secretly, he wanted to play again; realistically, he held little hope of that opportunity ever presenting itself.

Then, however, a call came from Baltimore's general manager. The season was in its sixth week, his old team was having defensive problems, and they wanted him back in the lineup. They would call back shortly to settle contract details and tell him which plane he should catch.

But, just minutes after the call, the phone rang again. It was Bill Arnsparger, defensive coordinator of the Miami Dolphins. "There's a plane out of Austin tomorrow morning at six," he said. "We need you here." Why he had suddenly become such a desired item, Lyle has no idea to this day. But, he sensed that the Dolphins wanted him urgently, and it felt good. He'd tried Baltimore and had left with uncomfortable feelings. Maybe it was best to try something new, go somewhere for yet another fresh start and leave the past behind.

Lyle talked with Suzanne, confiding to her how badly he still wanted to prove himself as a football player. She urged him to accept the Dolphins' offer; someone else could manage the restaurant.

Thirty minutes after he had boarded the plane to Miami, the Colts called to talk contract. They were too late. Lyle Blackwood was on his way to the success he'd been dreaming of since those schoolboy days back in San Antonio.

There was a lure to the Miami offer that went beyond the opportunity to play for a team with championship possibilities and one of the most highly regarded coaches in the game. Already on the Dolphins roster was Glenn Blackwood, Lyle's younger brother. Drafted in the eighth round in 1978, Glenn worked himself into the position of starting strong safety in Miami. Lyle, who would be tried at free safety, liked the idea of being a part of the only brother combination to start in the same defensive backfield.

So did Glenn.

For Glenn Blackwood, six years younger than Lyle, the trail to stardom had, at times, seemed almost too easy. A four-sport performer at the same high school where his brother had earned his letters, Glenn was the target of enthusiastic recruiting by college scouts. Although he weighed only 155 pounds, his aggressive style of play impressed all who watched him. And, too, there were those who realized they had made a mistake by not pursuing his older brother years before.

"We made a mistake on Lyle," said University of Texas head coach Darrell Royal, "because we felt he was just too small to play in the Southwest Conference. Then, he wound up at TCU and dealt us all kinds of misery for two years. We made up our minds that we weren't going to make that kind of mistake a second time."

For three years, Glenn was a starting cornerback for the University of Texas, ending his collegiate career on a team that spent most of the season ranked number one in the nation. When his eligibility was completed, he was drafted by the Dolphins and quickly established himself as one of the league's premier rookies.

It was while Glenn was a Dolphins rookie and Lyle was still with the Colts that the two brothers first met on the football field. And the results were nightmarish. Glenn, attempting to dodge a block by Lyle, landed awkwardly and damaged ligaments in his knee. But, there were no hard feelings.

"You have no idea how thrilled I was to learn that Lyle was going to join the Dolphins," Glenn said. "I'd like to be able to say that I went to Coach Shula and lobbied for him to give my brother a shot; but, hey, I was just a green rookie at the time and wasn't all that comfortable with my own position. I doubt they would have paid any attention to me even if I had said anything."

Lyle is still not altogether sure his younger brother is telling the truth on the matter. "I don't guess it's all that important," he says. "But I do know he was standing there at the airport when I arrived, ready to lend whatever support I needed.

"There was a time, frankly, when I was a pretty negative influence on Glenn. As a big brother, I should have known more, been able to give him some guidance, but I was into that live-for-today mentality at the time. Fortunately, for him, he has always had a mind of his own and probably wasn't as influenced by me as some younger brothers might have been. I'm thankful for that."

Glenn, while downplaying the negative influences of his brother, admits that he too went through a period of wild living. "But what happened to me was different from the problems Lyle had. Oh, I drank my share of beer, chased the ladies, things like that. But I never had the really hard times he had to deal with. I was more fortunate—I found God before Lyle did."

Glenn was still in high school when he became close friends with teammate Ted Constanzo. "In our senior year," he recalls, "Ted was the most highly recruited high-school quarterback in the nation. The guy had set all kinds of records and had his pick of schools. But what impressed me even more than his great athletic ability was the manner in which he dealt with all the attention and praise. It didn't seem to affect him in the least.

"One afternoon, we went fishing. As we were sitting there on the lake, I finally asked him the question I'd been wanting to for some time. I asked him what made him different from most of the really good athletes who seemed to have pretty inflated egos. Without the slightest hesitation, he turned to me and gave me a one-word answer, 'Christ.' That really made me stop and think about what God could mean to a person's life. I liked what I saw in Ted Constanzo, and I wanted to have the same confidence and peace of mind he obviously had."

In time, Glenn passed the same message on to his brother.

"By the time I got to Miami," says Lyle, "I was what you would have to call a struggling Christian. I was talking a pretty good game, but I still wasn't doing much of a job of practicing everything I preached. Glenn was a great help, even though he probably wasn't aware of it initially. I knew that he and his wife, Beth, were active Christians and wouldn't buy any hypocrisy from me. With Glenn watching, I knew I would have to start living the life I was talking about. In a very quiet way, Glenn helped me to begin doing that."

In a sense, then, it was the younger brother who challenged the elder.

Today, the Blackwood brothers are men on the same course, athletically as well as personally. One remains the more gregarious. It was Glenn who chose to inform the world of the birth of his daughter, Caitlin, last season by wearing a sticker announcing, "It's a girl," on his helmet during the AFC championship game. The other is more somber, but the strong bond between them is clearly visible. As members of the Dolphins secondary, they work together well, as if they can read each other's thoughts. As Christians, they each donate a great deal of time and energy in witnessing to youngsters.

Lyle, now the more seriously minded of the two, is quick to admit that his arrival in Miami signaled the start of a new life for him. "I had to learn things the hard way, I suppose. Glenn had a little more sense. Fortunately, he was able to deal with things in a grown-up manner, even before he was grown up. I've had a roller-coaster career. I've been cut, picked up, released, started, traded, and picked up again. I've been up and down—on really bad teams and on Super Bowl teams. Suzanne and I have been through rocky times and wonderful times. There were times when I felt it was me against the world. Now, we have three wonderful daughters who mean the world to me. With the help of God and a lot of people who care about me, I've made it to where I am today. I wouldn't want to go through a lot of it again, but I like to think maybe I'm a better person because of the experiences I've had."

Glenn has heard his brother's story time and time again at Christian rallies and never tires of it. "He's very candid about his life and is willing to share it with others. Lyle's living proof that a man can overcome all obstacles if he just works at it.

"The part I like best about his story is that it has such a happy ending."

Jim Ryun

Olympic Miler

IT WAS ONE OF THOSE magical, made-to-order days that seems rarely to come to the world of sports. Seldom had the weather been so cooperative, as if it were eager to do its part on an afternoon that was destined to go down in athletic history. California's late summer temperature stood at a comfortable seventy-five degrees, and there was but the slightest hint of wind. All in all, the conditions were ideal for an attempt on the world record for the mile run.

Young Jim Ryun—then a freshman at the University of Kansas—was already being hailed internationally as possibly the greatest miler in track and field history. He was going to attempt to return the world record for his specialty to the United States after a twenty-nine-year absence. Adding a touch of irony and anticipation to that July day in 1966 was the fact that the last American to set the record—Glenn Cunningham—had also been a student at Kansas.

Now had come Ryun, the nineteen-year-old running prodigy. A rail-thin Topeka, Kansas, native, he had bewildered the track world by running one mile in less than four minutes as a schoolboy. And he had earned a spot on the 1964 Olympic team. While still just a high-school junior, Ryun had already competed against and defeated most of the world's premier distance runners.

As a teenager, Ryun had run past athletic milestones with the same relaxed ease he displayed running past more experienced opponents. All that remained for him to be officially recognized as the best miler in the world was to break the record. And he had let it be known that this was the reason for his being in Berkeley, California, on that particular weekend.

Thus, this track and field meet had suddenly become one of the most eagerly awaited meets of the season. Just weeks earlier, the meet had faced the possibility of cancelation due to the lack of interest of both the fans and the competitors. Originally, it was to have matched the top American athletes against a national team from Poland. But the Poles, upset over the American involvement in Vietnam, had issued an eleventh-hour announcement that they were not coming. Meet sponsors were faced with financial disaster. They met in an emergency session and decided finally to go ahead with the meet, matching top American athletes against each other in the events. More important, since the meet would no longer boast an international flavor, officials decided to switch from the planned metric distances to yards, which were more familiar to American fans. Instead of the fifteen-hundred meters run, the program would include the mile run.

As soon as word of the switch from metric distances to yards reached Kansas, an excited Jim Ryun placed a long-distance call to meet director Sam Bell. "Mr. Bell," the modest youngster said, "I'd like to take a shot at the world record."

With that short, to-the-point conversation, the meet that had been floundering with the possibility of failure suddenly took on renewed importance. Of course, there would be a full complement of events standard to all track and field meets. And many of the greatest runners, throwers, and jumpers on the American scene would be on hand.

But Sam Bell knew that this particular day would be remembered for a single event. Years after the meet had passed into the history books, track and field enthusiasts would always remember what took place that day. It came to be known simply as "The Berkeley Mile"—one of the most incredible achievements in the carefully chronicled history of sports.

The crowd of fifteen thousand was buzzing with excitement as the entrants in the mile run were introduced: Cary Weisiger from the San Diego Track Club, who ran the mile in less than four minutes; Richard Romo, a University of Texas graduate who became the first Texan to break the four-minute barrier; Oklahoma State's Tom Von Ruden; Oregon's Wade Bell; and Pat Traynor, the veteran distance runner from the Forty-niners Track Club. Then, announcer Dwain Esper called attention to the lanky young man pulling off his sweat suit. An echoing ovation greeted Jim Ryun as he approached the starting line, seconds away from his bid for athletic immortality.

Each of the competitors played a part in the drama. All were aware of Ryun's goal and knew that a fast pace throughout the race would be of utmost importance. So they had agreed to help and planned to set a record pace through the first three-quarters of the race and let Ryun go the final lap on his own.

A sudden hush fell over the crowd as the starter called the runners to their marks. Then, at the crack of the gun, Von Ruden jumped into the lead with Ryun close on his heels. The runners sprinted effortlessly down the straightaway of the track. The cheering began, not to subside until the race was completed.

If a record was to be possible, Ryun would have to complete the first quarter-mile in fifty-eight seconds. Von Ruden, running as if a clock was plugged into his brain, paced his friend and rival through the first lap in 57.99 seconds. As the announcer reported the record pace, the fans burst out with renewed cheering, and Romo jumped into the lead to set the pace for the second lap. Ryun, still running effortlessly, matched him stride for stride.

He passed the half-mile mark in 1 minute, 55.5 seconds—still on schedule. Romo—his mission accomplished—relinquished the pace to Bell as the runners charged into the third lap.

Going into the backstretch, Ryun began to make his move, pushing himself to an even faster pace, past Bell and into the lead. Now he knew that it was up to him. In a field of six of the top American milers, Jim Ryun was now running all alone. For the final one and a half laps, it was a battle against agonizing fatigue and the stopwatch. The crowd cheered even louder as he gained a seven-yard lead over the talented field.

In the stands, they sensed a record in the making. None of those watching had ever seen a world record set in the mile—this was a spectacular event in American track. Fully aware that they were privileged witnesses to history, the fans yelled encouragement as Ryun drove down the backstretch. The noise almost drowned out the announcement of the time for three quarters; but those who did hear the time—2 minutes, 55.3 seconds—burst into screams. All that was needed now was a 58-second last lap—and the record would be broken. Famed for his last lap sprints, Ryun had never run his last quarter mile slower than 58 seconds in a major race.

As he entered the last lap, the competition was now falling far behind. Ryun found himself thinking that perhaps a 3:50 mile was possible—despite the pain that was setting in. His powerful legs were beginning to ache, his arms were becoming heavy, and his lungs were burning. Yet, almost incredibly, he stepped up the pace as the crowd rose to cheer him through the final tortuous lap. He pressed his pace around the curve, faster than usual because now every fraction of a second counted. This was no time to miss the record by a slight tick of the clock. He had come too far to fail.

With three hundred yards to go, he tried again to increase the pace, to go into the long homestretch sprint for which he had become famous. Digging deep into his physical and mental reserves, he couldn't find the hoped-for lift. The blistering early pace had taken its toll. There would be no blinding sprint for the tape this day—rather, just a struggle to maintain his current pace and not yield to the extreme fatigue that was engulfing his body.

As he came out of the last curve and into the final straightaway, there was little outward evidence of the pain. Four years of daily training in the early mornings of Kansas winters and the heat of sweltering summers had prepared him physically for this moment. Yet, there is no training program to make one ready for the kind of pain Ryun was feeling as he powered his way through the final yards of the race.

In the stands, people were jumping up and down, slapping each other on the back in premature celebration. Meet officials lined the track, waving their white caps and yelling encouragement.

Oblivious to all the commotion, Ryun drove his arms hard in long-reaching swings, pumping his weary legs until, at last, he was past the finish line. It was over! As wild celebration took over, he walked slowly around the curve—his head pounding, his legs aching. He was walking slowly down the backstretch when the official announcement came over the public address system: The time was 3 minutes, 51.3 seconds! The world record was back in America! A group of track experts calculated that Ryun had run the distance of eighteen yards faster than anyone had ever run before.

Meet officials asked him to take a victory lap, something he'd never felt comfortable doing before. Embarrassed, yet thrilled with his accomplishment, he jogged a lap barefoot, acknowledging the standing ovation with waves and a smile.

Within twenty-four hours, Ryun's victory was front-page news throughout the world. In Paris, a newspaper used two full pages to report the record race. TV's Walter Cronkite broke into regular programming with a bulletin just minutes after the race was completed. UPI sportswriter Joe Sargis wrote that "young Jim Ryun stood all alone today as perhaps the greatest track and field hero of all time."

Before the tumult and shouting died down, Ryun was given an award by the Amateur Athletic Union for the most outstanding single performance in the world for 1966. The Helms Athletic Foundation named him the outstanding amateur athlete in North

America. He also won—by the largest voting margin in the trophy's thirty-eight year history—the prestigious Sullivan Award as America's top amateur athlete.

Today, twenty years later, the achievement is still viewed by many as one of sport's greatest moments.

"Goals," Ryun says, "are worthwhile and the work necessary to achieve them is good for a person. I still find myself wondering, however, about the effects of reaching a goal like breaking a world record. All the attention, the press making you sound like some kind of a superhuman, people asking for your autograph. It's very easy to let your values get thrown out of balance."

This was, in fact, a problem that concerned him even as a schoolboy at East High in Wichita. When it became increasingly obvious that he was going to become the first high-school runner to break four minutes in the mile, Ryun went to his minister and asked him if he felt it was proper to pursue such a lofty goal. The answer was one that stayed with Ryun throughout his remarkable career.

"Jim," the minister told him, "if you don't set your goals high, you're never going to realize the full potential of the talents God has blessed you with. If you are going into the sort of thing you've chosen, if you're going to try to develop into the greatest miler in the world, then you, as a Christian, must dedicate yourself to doing the very best you can.

"Just don't ever get to the point where you feel you can achieve greatness alone. Remember that you have to have God's help."

"I was seventeen when he told me that," Ryun says. "I understood what he was telling me, even then. But, as I grew older, it made even more sense. Running has been a big part of my life. It has brought me a great deal of personal satisfaction. I was able to travel all over the world to compete. And I achieved some things: I've reached some goals I'd set for myself. Still it is not a truly lasting thing. Records get broken. Someone faster will always come along and get the attention of the press. I will always consider running an important and satisfying part of my life. But not as important as the lasting things—my Christian faith and my family."

*   *   *

In the years that followed the Berkeley Mile, Jim Ryun's athletic career developed into one with peaks and valleys. In June of 1967, he lowered his own world record to 3:51.1. The following year, however, competing in Mexico City's devastating one and one-half mile altitude, he fell short in his bid to win the gold medal in the Olympics. In the fifteen hundred meters race, he finished second to Kenya's Kipchoge Keino. He stunned the track world in 1969 by stepping off the track, failing to finish his race in the National AAU championships in Miami. "My priorities are changing too fast for me to keep up with them," the weary Ryun told reporters. "Suddenly, I no longer feel capable of or interested in running."

Discouraged by a long list of minor yet nagging injuries that had been plaguing him, he was also miffed by the sudden sharp criticism from the media. Facing new responsibilities as a husband, Ryun announced his retirement at a time when many felt he should be at the peak of his career. It was impossible to believe that Jim Ryun—the teenage folk hero, the soft-spoken young man who had brought his sport into the national spotlight—would never run again.

His retirement lasted nineteen months. In retrospect, the complex young man admitted he had created unbearable pressures on himself. "People," he later said, "had made me a superhuman, and I felt I had to constantly push myself to be that imaginary person."

It was not the constant urging of friends or his long-time coach Bob Timmons, or even his own personal desire to complete unfinished business, that eventually compelled him to start training again. That credit goes to his wife, Anne, a pretty former Kansas State coed whom Ryun met while competing in track meets on the KSU campus.

"When Jim decided to give up running, he was very unhappy," she recalls. "But after a while, he realized that not running was making him even more unhappy. What he had to do was to make up his mind that he would forget the outside pressures and not worry about the demands of others."

"I had always felt that I had a God-given talent and a responsibility to develop it," Ryun says. "So I thought about it and prayed about it. I asked God to show me the best way to return to athletics. I also asked that he give me the strength to face the pressures I had allowed to build up in my mind."

Thus, in January of 1971, he resumed training and worked with the same dedication and enthusiasm he had displayed as a teenager. Still, he continued to falter in competitions. For every good race he ran, there were two bad ones in which he had run poorly or had not even finished.

In an attempt to work himself back into top condition, he moved to Eugene, Oregon, the home base of many top distance runners in the nation. The relocation only created new problems. The high pollen count wreaked havoc with Ryun's allergies, causing him to lose a great amount of workout time.

Ryun's next stop was Santa Barbara, California. Still, things weren't falling into place. He continued to struggle but seldom showed any competitive sign of the Jim Ryun of old. Early in 1972, a new Olympic year, he placed last in the Meet of Champions in Los Angeles. Jim ran the mile distance in 4 minutes, 19 seconds—slower than any time he had posted since his sophomore year in high school.

The Ryuns moved back to Kansas. "I kept thinking that it might be my last chance to try for an Olympic gold medal," he remembers. "So I decided to go back to my old coach and my old surroundings and see if that might help."

It did. Slowly but surely, Ryun began rounding into shape. The allergy problems disappeared and his old confidence began to return. Eventually, he qualified for his third trip to the Olympic Games by winning the fifteen hundred meters in the American team trials. At last, things were again looking up. Jim Ryun, in top form and running well, appeared ready to accomplish the one goal that he had failed to achieve in two previous Olympics.

Then, in Munich, Germany, came the ultimate frustration. In a qualifying heat, Ryun tried to pass two runners late in the third lap of the race. With about five hundred meters to go, a tiring Mohammed Younis of Pakistan accidentally moved into the American runner. His arm struck Ryun in the torso. Ryun stumbled backward into Billy Fordjour of Ghana. As they fell, Fordjour's knee struck Ryun's throat and jaw, causing him to lose his breath. The fall also resulted in an injury to Ryun's hip and strained his right knee and left ankle. Ryun lay on his back for several agonizing seconds; then, he courageously got to his feet and completed the race. Far back among the finishers, however, his time was not good enough to advance him to the finals.

Standing on the infield, his knee bleeding and his vision blurred by pain and tears, Jim Ryun was faced with the realization that his last hope for an Olympic gold medal was gone. Once again disappointed and disillusioned, he began to ponder the end of his athletic career.

"When I left Munich," he recalls, "we had $200 in the bank. And I had no real idea of what I was going to do for a living when I got home. You can't imagine how guilty I felt. Anne, who had been teaching school to support us while I trained, was pregnant. All I could think about was the need for me to forget competing and find a way to make us financially secure."

Briefly, he considered pursuing photography as a career. This was something he had enjoyed as a hobby. But a call came from a man named Michael O'Hara, a former Olympic volleyball player and successful California businessman. He told Ryun that he was forming an organization called the International Track Association. O'Hara was convinced that this country was ready to accept the concept of professional track. But what it needed to succeed was a headliner, a name star who could capture the attention of the fans being introduced to the new professional sport.

Suddenly, the roller-coaster life of Jim Ryun was taking another upward swing. What O'Hara and pro track were offering was the best of two worlds. Ryun could continue his competitive career and, at the same time, insure a handsome income for his family.

He signed a contract that called for a bonus as well as a regular salary for his promotional services on behalf of the International Track Association. Additionally, there would be the prize money waiting in the forty meets on the pro circuit.

It appeared that the formation and brief success of the pro-track circuit caused a transformation in Jim Ryun. Relaxed, he seemed to delight in referring to himself as a "professional jock." At age twenty-six, the sports' world phenomenon finally became comfortable with himself.

"For years," he says, "I devoted my entire life, all of my energies, to running, training, and competing. I missed a lot of things, a lot of the simple pleasures of day-to-day living. But I finally realized that it was no sin to relax and enjoy things now and then. And once I recognized that, with God's help, a lot of the pressures were gone forever."

In time, Ryun again found the demands of training and traveling more than he wanted to deal with. An Achilles' heel problem made practice difficult. And there were gentle hints from Anne that perhaps it was time to turn his energies in new directions. Comfortable with the accomplishments of his career, he began again to contemplate retirement. This time, however, it would be for the right reasons.

On a March afternoon in 1976, he called a news conference in the press room at the University of Kansas. With several dozen members of the media on hand, he thanked them for coming.

"You know," he began, "we've been through a lot for the last twelve or thirteen years. There's been ups and downs. And I just want each of you to know how much I've appreciated your kindness toward me. But now I've got something to tell you that is probably going to sound a little unusual.

"God blessed me with an ability to do some things others were unable to do. Why he picked me to be a successful runner, I'll never really know. But I'm so thankful that he did. It's been a wonderful life. But, for some time now, I've been contemplating what I will do with the remainder of my life. The other evening, as I lay in bed, the Lord spoke to me. It is my firm conviction that he told me it is time to retire. He said, 'You've run a good race; you've fought a good fight. Now it's finished. I have something more for you.' "

The announcement was made with a smile, a cheerfulness that suggested no apologies.

That was ten years ago. Since then, there have been two more Olympic Games celebrated. The world mile-record has been improved a dozen or more times. And new stars have emerged on the distance-running scene. Still, however, the name Jim Ryun retains a magical ring. Few so young, so gifted, so dedicated have done the things he accomplished on the athletic field. In a sense, Ryun was a pioneer. He opened the door for those who would follow, making dreams of faster, previously unheard-of, times possible.

Today, at age thirty-seven, Jim is once again running—not

on the track, but on the roads in ten kilometer runs. One day, he says, he might even try a marathon. He no longer runs to set records or, for that matter, even to win. Today, running is fun—something it rarely was during those highly competitive days when the world expected him to burst through new barriers every time he stepped on the track.

Jim Ryun is a man at peace. Living in Lawrence, Kansas, with Anne and their four children, he is more relaxed, more easy-going than he was that long ago day when he was a freshman college student.

"I grew up in a Christian environment and always considered myself a Christian," he says. "But it was not until I decided finally to give up competitive running, to cut myself loose from a way of life I'd been involved in for thirteen years—that I began to learn about myself and my Christianity.

"For a lot of years I was pretty self-centered. I ran for myself. I knew God had given me the talent and the stamina, but I never actually ran for him. Only when I retired, not knowing what I would do to support my family, did I really give myself over to him. It was then that I finally put my fate in God's hands and really turned my life over to him."

Now Jim shares his religious convictions with runners throughout the country. There are Jim Ryun Running Camps where athletic hopefuls, young and old alike, come to hear the three-time Olympian offer training tips and spiritual advice. Motivational seminars conducted by Ryun have also changed the lives of thousands.

And he runs with a new joy, a new purpose. "I'm no longer the fastest miler in the world. I don't need to be. Today, I run with a new desire to share Jesus Christ and his wonderful, obedient, disciplined lifestyle. Running with Jesus has brought me the freedom and happiness that running for myself never could."

And this, he says, is worth more than even an Olympic gold medal!

Darrell Porter

Catcher, Texas Rangers

IT BEGAN AS ONE OF those too-good-to-be-true kind of stories upon which athletic legends are built. Darrell Porter, one of four gifted athletes in the Porter family of Oklahoma City, seemed born to greatness. From those first days as a catcher and a pitcher for the Pee Wee League Davis Mustangs, he was an athlete who stood above his peers. By the time he had graduated from Southeast High School, he had inherited the starting quarterback job on the football team from his older brother. Darrell was an All-State guard in basketball and was twice voted the state's premier schoolboy baseball player.

No less than thirty-five colleges—including home state powerhouse Oklahoma—praised his strong passing arm and offered him football scholarships. Then, the Milwaukee Brewers stepped forward, offering Porter instant wealth—a $70,000 bonus to by-pass college and take a shot at becoming a major league catcher.

After less than two years in the minor leagues, he made it and earned a place on the Milwaukee roster. He was living proof that the "All-American Boy" syndrome was alive and well.

Darrell Porter, gifted athlete, church-goer—the kid who was generally assigned the job of "driver," since he refused to drink beer when his celebrating high-school teammates did—had it all. He married, his baseball prowess continued to improve, and he climbed to the rank of All-Star catcher.

To those who knew him only from a grandstand vantage point or from what they read in the newspapers, Darrell Porter was one of those blessed people who had the world by a string.

This was the public man. In private, he was on an aimless, destructive course. In truth, Darrell Porter could not cope with the life he was leading. The only reality, it seemed, was baseball. Away from the ball park, he was a man lacking in confidence and inner strength. He tried to drown those shortcomings in booze or escape them with the mind-blur of drugs. In time, his marriage failed, his friends began to disappear, and he gained a reputation as one of the game's most volatile, aggressive players—big league baseball's answer to the angry young man.

More than once, while passing the agonizing hours before game time in a strange hotel room, he stared out the window, wondering if he should step onto the ledge and jump. On one occasion, he admits, he went so far as to stick the barrel of a pistol in his mouth.

Still, many knew him only as a man with a solid batting average and the uncanny ability to throw out runners at second base. No one had any idea of the inner torment with which he was dealing.

It was in the spring of 1980, with a new season about to

begin, that the dark pressures finally overwhelmed Porter. As
he reported to Fort Myers, Florida, for spring training with the
Kansas City Royals (the team he had been traded to in 1977),
he was a man ill-prepared for the job. Paranoid and angry, he
could not even feel the warmth of the Florida sun. In the winter
months that preceded his arrival, he had worked out a little
and snorted cocaine a lot. He was not ready to meet the challenges
of a new season, physically or mentally. He knew he needed
help but wasn't sure where to turn.

The Royals had been training just over a week when Don
Newcombe, the former Dodgers pitcher, arrived in Fort Myers
to speak to the team. He told of how drinking had shortened
his career and all but ruined his life. In the moving talk—which
he gives to teams throughout professional baseball—Newcombe
gave a quiet but effective testimony, admitting that only through
the grace of God and Alcoholics Anonymous was he able to
get sober and rebuild his life.

At the end of his talk, he passed out a sheet with fifteen
questions. "If you are able to answer as many as three of them
with a yes," he told his audience, "you have a drinking problem."

Though Newcombe's talk dealt primarily with drinking,
Porter saw similarities to the problems the speaker reflected on
and those he was having. When he completed the questionnaire,
Darrell Porter found that he had answered fourteen of the questions positively. And, for the first time, he admitted to himself
that he was an addict—to booze and drugs. The next step was
to talk with Newcombe. Admitting his problem, Porter knew,
would not be easy, but certainly someone like Newcombe, who
had endured much of the same mind torture he'd experienced,
would understand and be sympathetic.

Newcombe did understand; but he was far from sympathetic.
He listened to Darrell's admission that he had not only been
drinking heavily but had been taking a variety of drugs for the
past eight years. Then, the former pitcher rose, glared, and said,
"Porter, you're a disgrace to the uniform you're wearing. There
are thousands of kids out there looking up to you, wanting to
grow up to be like you in every way they can. And you're sitting
there telling me you're an alcoholic and a drug addict. You're
a real idiot."

The reaction was far from what Porter had expected. Still,

he followed Newcombe's advice and went to club president Joe Burke and told him of his problem.

Burke, like Newcombe, was stunned that his number one catcher—a man who had hit 20 home runs and driven in 112 runs just the season before—was admitting to an addiction to drugs. Disappointed and angry, he finally said there was no way that he could allow Porter to play for the Royals until the problem was resolved.

Even as Burke and Porter were talking, Newcombe was making arrangements for the All-Star catcher to be admitted to The Meadows, a drug rehabilitation clinic in Wickenburg, Arizona.

Porter's emotions ran the gamut from relief to humiliation. Finally, he felt, he had a chance to beat the problem that had so long tortured him. But he also realized that the public would soon know he was something less than what the sports page write-ups had made him out to be. His family and friends would be hurt when his drug problem became public knowledge. And, no doubt, there would be fans who would never again cheer his efforts. And, most frightening, there was no guarantee that the program offered at The Meadows would work. If it didn't— if he wasn't given medical clearance at the end of his stay—his career in baseball might be over.

He wondered how had he allowed himself to jeopardize his career, his life, in such a manner.

It began rather innocently one cool summer night in Appleton, Wisconsin. Assigned to the minor league Clinton Pilots in Iowa, the youthful Darrell Porter was having great difficulty adjusting to life away from home. Still uncertain that he even wanted to play professional baseball, he was younger than most of his teammates and saw himself as an outcast. Bashful, he seldom talked with the other players, never attended their postgame parties, and had no social life. In those first weeks in the minors, he was either at the ball park playing, on the bus to the next town, or alone in his room feeling homesick and miserable.

Things went from bad to worse when he fell into a hitting slump that stretched over a two-week period. His misery was compounded.

"All through Little League and high school," he remembers,

"I was the best player on the team. I never lacked confidence. Then, when I went to the pros, I found myself playing with guys older and more experienced than I was. It was a frightening experience. I was lonely and disappointed in my performance. I wasn't measuring up and wondered why I had even considered playing pro ball."

One evening, after another dismal night at the plate, Porter was approached by several of his teammates who recognized the pressures he was struggling with. They insisted that he join them for a couple of beers. It would, they promised, help him get his mind off his problems.

Having grown up with an alcoholic father, Porter had vowed never to drink. He had surrendered his life to Christ during his high-school days and had been an active member of the Wilmont Baptist Church in Oklahoma City. Darrell prayed regularly that God might give him strength to be the kind of person he wanted him to be.

But the pressure of his teammates, compounded by the despair he was feeling, resulted in his accepting the invitation to "have a few beers and unwind."

"That night," Darrell recalls, "I got really drunk. The more I drank, the better I felt. I was no longer shy or feeling sorry for myself. I felt a part of the group for the first time and enjoyed it. I didn't feel homesick or lonely anymore. I even talked with several girls there in the bar. It was great. I had found an escape."

In the days to come, he took advantage of the alcoholic escape more and more regularly. A year later, he advanced to marijuana.

"I was playing winter ball," he says, "and some of the guys had me over one night and introduced me to pot. I was hesitant at first, but again, I was too weak to say no. And then, after I'd tried it and experienced the high, I found I liked the feeling. I liked laughing at everything and being so relaxed."

In time, however, the laughter died. Booze and drugs became more than a happy escape; they became a day-to-day need. And that need began to erode the quality of young Darrell Porter's life.

His marriage to his teenage sweetheart broke up in 1974 in a wash of anger and suspicion. Ironically, it was the same year he was selected to catch in the All-Star game. Soon beer and pot weren't enough; next came Quaaludes, then cocaine. "I was willing to do anything to block out the pain of the divorce," he says. "I used the drugs to set up a barrier that blocked out my feelings. The thing I didn't realize at the time was that the drugs not only blocked out the pain but the chance of happiness as well."

But even as his drug dependency became more and more serious, Darrell Porter continued to climb the professional baseball ladder. The Brewers called him late in the 1971 season and, for the next six years, he established himself as one of baseball's premier catchers. His sport was fast becoming his only reality. Only at the ball park on game day did Darrell Porter feel his life had real meaning.

In time, however, Porter's private misery began making its way onto the playing field. More reclusive than ever, he avoided his teammates except in the dressing room and on the field. More and more, he was involved in fights during games. What some viewed as nothing more than aggressive play was actually his hostility and frustration acted out in front of thousands of cheering fans. Though he held onto his starting job, Porter's contribution was far shy of what management had expected. There were too many wild throws to second base, allowing too many stolen bases. In 1976, his batting average fell to .208.

The promise of greatness, once proclaimed so loudly, had dwindled to a hopeful whisper. Before the 1977 season got underway, Porter received word that he had been traded to Kansas City.

"It was a big disappointment to me," he says. "But I look back on those last two years with Milwaukee, and they're all fuzzy and out of focus. I can't remember much of anything. I know I must have acted weird and had people wondering about me. But I honestly don't think anyone really knew what my problem was. That's the way it is in baseball. If a guy's acting nutty, you leave him alone. Live and let live; unfortunately, that's the credo."

Once the reality of the trade finally soaked in, Porter began to view the move to Kansas City as an opportunity for a new start. Whitey Herzog, the Royals manager, believed in him. And there was a camaraderie on the Kansas City team which had been absent in Milwaukee. "I saw the move as an opportunity to reestablish myself," Porter says. "I made up my mind to go to spring training and work my tail off and see just how good a ballplayer I could be."

This determination, however, did not include the decision to break away from his drug habit. Rather, he rationalized a new approach—no Quaaludes or pot before a game; cocaine would be restricted to the off-season.

"I really thought I was smart, that I had it all worked out," he says. "But all I was doing was making a bigger fool of myself. I knew that the drugs were beginning to affect my playing; but, rather than stop cold turkey, I thought I could beat it by putting myself on a schedule. This, probably as much as anything, should have told me that I really had problems, that I was no longer thinking straight."

While Darrell Porter's private life continued a downward spiral, his play on the field improved remarkably in his first season with the Royals. His batting average climbed to .275. He hit sixteen home runs and accounted for sixty runs-batted-in, helping his new team into the American League playoffs. They were eliminated by the New York Yankees, but the season had promised a bright future for Kansas City. And many were saying that the real catalyst for success was the emergence of Porter.

When the 1978 season began, he was again in the spotlight— selected as the Player of the Month in April, hitting well, and reducing the number of errors he'd made the season before. Having confined much of his drug usage to the off-season, Darrell was more alert and in better physical condition than he'd been in several years.

A year later—in his third season with the Royals—Porter was selected as the American League's starting catcher in the All-Star game. His batting average climbed to .291. He was the toast of the Kansas City baseball world. His own world, however, was again falling apart. Despite a $150,000-per-year salary, he found himself in financial troubles. Back taxes were owed the Internal Revenue Service, and several business ventures had turned sour.

By the time the season ended, Darrell was in the worst mental state of his life. Drugs dominated his waking hours and paranoia mounted. He was sure the Royals management knew about his drug habit and was having him followed. Even a trip to the supermarket became a harrowing experience as fear of arrest gripped him. At night, he would sit watching through a darkened window for imaginary undercover spies, his hunting gun resting in his lap. When he did finally go to bed, he slept with a baseball bat at arm's reach so that he might defend himself against intruders, whom he was certain were coming after him.

Such were the depths one of the game's most celebrated players had reached. It was a sense of panic that eventually motivated him to seek out Don Newcombe and admit his problems. "There was just no way I could continue going to the ball park with a phony smile on my face. It was a crazy smile. There I was, coming off my greatest season in baseball, and I was miserable—and scared. I found myself thinking a lot about dying."

Those first weeks at The Meadows provided Porter with a new kind of challenge. He met alcoholic businessmen, wealthy women who actually smuggled pills into the facility that was trying to offer them help, and administrators who were not in the least impressed with the fact that he was one of major league baseball's superstars. Out there, he was told, he might be a highly paid, successful ballplayer; but at The Meadows, he was nothing more than another drug addict.

Initially, he rebelled at the personal probing of staff members into his personal life. The group therapy sessions annoyed him. And the idea of keeping a daily journal seemed childish. Still, he tried to fit into the program, to convince himself that the only solution to his problem was to comply with the demands of those charged with his care.

"It was a totally different world for me," he admits. "All my life I had felt I was in control, yet now I was being told that I wasn't. I was forced to take a long, hard look at my personal shortcomings and think about ways to do something about them."

One of the most crushing blows he felt during the early stages of his stay came when he read a headline in *The Sporting News:* PORTER ON DRUGS. His father, a man who admittedly had pushed him from childhood to become something he could not be, had granted an interview to a reporter and told of his son's drug problems.

"I guess I felt that if I couldn't amount to anything," the

elder Porter was quoted as saying, "I'd make sure my sons did. I drove Darrell into the ground. I never patted him on the back for his accomplishments. Instead, I kicked him in the rear to do better. I told Darrell a lot of times that he'd better be good at sports, because he wasn't worth a flip at anything else."

"I was hurt and angry when I read that story," Darrell says. "I felt my own father had betrayed me."

In time, the father and son confronted their differences at The Meadows. During a family day visit, which is part of the clinic's rehabilitation program, the two Porters sat face to face in a tension-filled session that brought out into the open old angers and hurts. Darrell yelled at his father, and his father yelled back as counselors encouraged them to clear the air, to speak out on things too long kept inside.

"It was one of the most emotionally draining experiences in my life," the younger Porter says. "We said a lot of hurtful things to each other, and we both cried. But when it was all over, we hugged each other. And, most important, we told each other that we loved one another."

The letters of encouragement he had received from friends and fans had helped in his resolve to beat his addiction, Porter admits. So had the fact that he had cleared the air with his father. It was, however, another realization that provided him his greatest source of strength.

"In my heart I knew if I was ever going to get straightened out and be happy again, it was going to be through Christ. I knew I was too weak to accomplish what I needed to by myself.

"It may sound strange, but through all my problems I had never really given up on Christ. I knew he was real. I never stopped going to our baseball chapel meetings, for instance. But I had become too weak to admit to myself that God could—and would—help me if only I made the effort to try and help myself.

"While I was there at The Meadows, I realized how badly I wanted God back in my life. I wanted the feelings (feelings that had since dried up) that I had in the Wilmont Baptist Church in Oklahoma City to come back, so I prayed and read the Bible daily.

"In a way, I was working as hard at reestablishing my contact with God as I was trying to rid myself of my drug problem."

A verse he found one evening while he was idly reading through the Bible provided Darrell the strength and determination necessary to reach his goal: "And ye shall seek me, and find *me,* when ye shall search for me with all your heart" (Jer. 29:13, KJV).

Six weeks had passed, and the season was nearing when Darrell Porter was pronounced well enough to leave the clinic and try to regain his spot with the Kansas City Royals. Fellow patients and staff members wished him well, and he was given a small medallion with the serenity prayer inscribed on it. It read: "God grant me the serenity to accept the things I cannot change, courage to change the things I can, and wisdom to know the difference."

It was on April 20, 1980, that Darrell Porter reported back to the Kansas City Royals. Reading a prepared statement to his teammates and members of the press, he said, "I am very happy to be back. Six weeks ago, God gave me the strength, courage, and determination to face up to my personal problems and to seek professional help. I went to Joe Burke and advised him that I was a drug addict and an alcoholic. My whole life has been affected. I have hurt my family, my friends, the great baseball fans of the Royals, my teammates, and I almost destroyed myself.

"For the past six weeks, the doctors, the counselors, and the staff at The Meadows have made me realize the most important things we have on our side is our lives and good health. With their help, I have a greater understanding and appreciation of myself and my responsibilities. I have been successfully treated, and I graduated this afternoon.

"I will always be grateful and thankful to those who prayed for me, sent letters of encouragement, and supported me. From this day forward, I will be facing the greatest challenge of my life. I am confident that with the help of God and your support and understanding I will be successful."

The welcome he received upon his return home stunned Porter. Yellow ribbons were tied on the trees along the block where he lived. In the stands, people cheered his arrival in the batting cage, waving signs that read, "Welcome Back, Darrell." In his first official at-bat, twenty-five thousand people, many of them wearing yellow ribbons at the suggestion of a local radio announcer, gave him a standing ovation that delayed play for several minutes.

Darrell Porter backed out of the batter's box, took off his hat, and made no attempt to hide the tears. Though doctors had told him it would be a year to eighteen months before he would totally regain his health, Porter knew he was on the road to recovery.

Though Porter was not in the best of shape, he managed to hit .249 during a season when the Royals won the American League title and a spot in the World Series against Philadelphia. In the Series, he went hitless and heard the inevitable rumors— false though they were—that he had again fallen off the wagon. And, in the aftermath of the Royals failure in the Series, there were rumors of trades. Several players, sportswriters were speculating, would not be back with the Royals the following year. Porter, whose play had been erratic most of the year, would probably be among the castoffs.

In time, the Royals did offer him a contract, but it was far short of what he should be paid.

Opting for free agency, he eventually signed a five-year contract with the St. Louis Cardinals. Once again he was looking at a new start. This time, however, he was not playing mind games with himself. His past, he knew full well, made him a gamble. Even the St. Louis reporters said so. But an old friend, Whitey Herzog, now managing the Cardinals, felt Porter was the man he needed to turn his team into a pennant winner.

No yellow ribbons awaited Porter's arrival in St. Louis. Fans were disgruntled over Herzog's decision to trade popular catcher Ted Simmons to Milwaukee, thus making a place for Porter in the Cardinals' lineup. Herzog, who had managed Porter for three years while with the Royals, answered his critics by saying that "he's a good money player, handles pitchers well, and the team he played for before coming here had the best record in its division four of the five years he caught for it."

Still, the fans came down hard on the Cardinals' new catcher. Some teammates silently wondered if Porter might crack under such pressure, considering the fact that he'd had problems in almost ideal conditions in Kansas City.

All of this showed they had not come to know the "new" Darrell Porter very well. He had remarried and become a father, had a lakefront home he enjoyed a great deal, was a witnessing Christian, and was confident that he would eventually win the hearts of fans in his new setting.

In his second season, he did just that.

On a team that included such standouts as Ozzie Smith, Bruce Sutter, Keith Hernandez, and George Hendricks, it was Darrell Porter who emerged as the star as the Cardinals won the World Series in seven games over the Milwaukee Brewers. Having already been named the Most Valuable Player in the National League championship series, Porter continued his play-off heroics with an impressive overall performance in the Series. He became the first player in World Series history to have two four-hit games. He accounted for five RBIs and had a home run. Defensively, he was flawless.

In the Cardinals dressing room, following the seventh and deciding game, teammates celebrated, dousing each other with champagne—except for Darrell Porter. He joked about it. "Don't even spray that stuff in my direction," he said. "Some of it might get in my pores, and there I'd go again. As long as it's been since I've had a drink, it wouldn't take much to get me drunk."

Even such a milestone as being the Most Valuable Player in the World Series is no just cause for risking a return to the way things used to be.

In his fourteenth season and looking toward the end of his career, Porter says baseball is now fun for him. This hasn't always been the case, even in more youthful times when his batting average was higher and injuries came less often.

"Since I got myself straightened out," he says, "the game has been fun. Even on some days when we lose, I stop and think how enjoyable it is just to be out there, feeling good.

"For a long time, I let drugs take away a lot of the enjoyment I should have been feeling. Drugs nearly killed me. It's only by the grace of God they didn't."

Prior to the 1986 season, Darrell Porter, at age thirty-four, was released by the Cardinals after a five-year stay in St. Louis. Once again a free agent, but convinced he still had some good years left in baseball, he signed with the Texas Rangers and began looking forward to his sixteenth season in the major leagues.

Cleveland Williams

Boxer

IT WAS A BRITTLE cold November night, which occasionally grips the Texas Gulf Coast, and Cleveland Williams—affectionately called "The Big Cat" by Houston's fight fans—was driving. Life looked good, the future held great promise; he had friends with him, and there was relaxed laughter in the companionship. The lonely Texas road, inviting and stretching far in front of him, was all but deserted. Williams stepped on the gas, feeling the warm sensation from the surge of power the automobile delivered.

Thus began one of the most incredible incidents in the history of professional sports. This is the story of a promising heavyweight with a big money future who, on that long ago night of November 28, 1964, was given up for dead three times while lying on the operating table of a charity hospital.

A shot from a Texas Highway Patrol officer's .357 magnum, fired from point-blank range, echoed through the pitch-black Texas night, sending Williams crumpling to the graveled roadside. It was a fleeting, bizarre, horror-filled moment that completely rearranged his life.

While the facts remain muddled in a mixture of Williams's semiconscious recollections and sketchy police reports, this is the account of the event which highway patrol officials and Williams most nearly agree on.

An officer stopped Williams's speeding car and, upon learning that the driver had been drinking, arrested him, ordering him into the patrol car. Williams, cocky and confident in the knowledge that his manager would bail him out when he reached the Houston city jail, made no effort to resist. Until, that is, the patrolman turned his car in the direction of nearby Tomball, Texas, instead of Houston.

A small community with an infamous reputation for its shoddy treatment of blacks in those days, Tomball was no place for even a celebrity like Cleveland Williams. He told the officer his fears as he grabbed at the door handle. The officer, fearful that his prisoner might escape, reached for Williams as he brought the car to a screeching halt. They continued to scuffle outside the car.

The officer then pulled his gun, and Williams, now frightened, made a desperate swing at it. Suddenly, the darkness was lit by the sudden explosion of the fired magnum. The bullet ripped crosswise through Williams's intestines, one of his kidneys, and lodged against his hip bone.

As the highway patrol officer stood, stunned and shaken, Cleveland Williams fell to the ground, a gaping hole in his side gushing blood. By all rights and medical reasoning, he should have been dead in a matter of minutes.

In that horrifying flash, Cleveland Williams's world crumbled. Regarded by many as the premier heavyweight contender in the world in 1964, he had been training for a fight with an equally talented up-and-comer named Cassius Clay. Their fight was to be an elimination bout, part of a tournament that would eventually decide who would claim the then vacant world heavyweight championship. The fight with Clay, however, was postponed because Clay had suffered an injury in training. Aware that he would have more time to prepare for the upcoming bout, Williams decided to slack off on his own training. On that November Saturday night, he decided to relax for a while, have a few beers, see some friends, and get away from training camp for the first time in over a month.

Then, suddenly, he was sprawled in the gravel, bleeding—dying.

Dr. Don C. Quast, a friend of Williams, was standing ready to perform surgery as they wheeled the dying boxer into the emergency room of Houston's famed Ben Taub General Hospital. He went immediately to work, laboring into the early morning hours, fighting what he remembers today as "a battle I felt I really had no chance of winning." Vital life signs were nonexistent on three different occasions during the course of the operation. The boxer's kidneys stopped functioning, and partial paralysis was evident in some of the hip muscles. The most optimistic outlook was that if, by some miracle, Williams should live, he would be paralyzed for the remainder of his life.

Even after Williams's remarkable survival of the crisis, there were three more delicate operations during a seven-month period, during which he lost sixty-two pounds. Still, doctors gradually became increasingly optimistic that they could eventually repair the massive destruction caused by the .357 magnum.

"The only thing that saved Cleve's life," says Dr. Quast, "was the fact that his abdominal wall was two to three times thicker than that of a normal person. The muscles that he had developed as a boxer literally slowed the bullet as it entered his body."

Members of the medical community marveled at the fact that Williams survived. None would go so far as to even hint that he might one day step back into the ring. Collectively, they underestimated the determination of Cleveland Williams.

"Looking back," he says, his face bearing evidence of over one hundred fights in a twenty-six-year career, "that night on that dark Texas road was the best thing that ever happened to me. It brought me closer to God, showed me who he really was. My whole life changed for the better after that experience."

Settling back in the living room of his Houston home, a smile tracing his contentment, he says, "I used to run around, drink, smoke. Everything I did was wrong. But no more. The Bible says, 'The wise man will change and the fool never does.' I've never thought of myself as a fool. I've got a life now that has meaning, all because I nearly had no life at all.

"That night in the hospital I wasn't really aware of much that was going on. But I did feel the miracle of God rushing through my left leg. I can remember it as clearly as if it were yesterday. I was never supposed to walk again, much less fight.

"God must have wanted me to fight because he gave me the gift. That's why I worked so hard to make a comeback. If God hadn't wanted me to continue with my boxing career, he would have let me die on that operating table like everyone thought I was going to do. He let me live and get well so I could fight again because, at the time, it was the only thing I knew."

Such had been the case since his boyhood days in a dirt-poor section of Griffin, Georgia. Cleveland dropped out of school in the seventh grade to go to work in the pulp mills to support his mother and grandmother, the only family he ever knew as a youngster.

It was a brutal life for a young boy, one of long hours in the company of hard men. Seldom did a day at the mills pass without at least one fistfight breaking out. And more often than not, one of the parties involved was young Cleveland Williams.

Encouraged by some men whose names he can no longer even recall, Williams, at age fourteen, became a professional fighter. He battled older, seedy club fighters from the bottom of the boxing barrel for nickle-and-dime purses.

"I looked a lot older than I really was," he says. "I was six feet tall and weighed something like 185 pounds. I won four of my fights by knockouts, lost one, and had one draw before somebody found out how old I was. As soon as they discovered my real age, I was barred from the sport until I reached my eighteenth birthday."

It was a lifetime wait for a money-hungry young boy who had found something he not only did well but which paid considerably better than the sweating, fruitless work at the pulp mills.

In 1951, he was reading a copy of a boxing magazine and came upon a story about the career of Florida-based boxing manager Lou Viscusi. "He sounded like a real smart manager," says Williams. "So I called him and told him I wanted to be a fighter and wanted him to be my manager. I'm sure he thought I was nuts, but he played along with me. He told me if I ever got down to Tampa to drop by and let him have a look at me. I'm sure he never expected to hear from me again."

Cleveland Williams took the next bus to Florida.

Under the guidance of Viscusi and trainer Bill Gore, Williams's career began anew in December of 1951 and, by the end of '52, he had won twenty-one fights, twenty of them by knockouts. His bruising punches were fast gaining him a reputation, and it took precious little time for the boxing community to recognize him as a legitimate title contender. Twice, he fought and eventually lost to world heavyweight champion Sonny Liston. The 1959 bout saw Liston decked with a broken nose before coming back to win the judges' decision.

Then in January of 1963 came the word that Houston Oilers owner Bud Adams and promoter Hugh Benbow had formed an organization called A and B Boxing Enterprises, Inc., and had purchased Williams's contract from Viscusi. Benbow had not only convinced football-minded Adams that Williams had the ability to become the world heavyweight champion but successfully talked him into financing most of the venture as well.

Adams's money purchased the contract, it paid Benbow $1,000-a-month salary, financed the remodeling of an old downtown building for a training gym, and provided Williams with living expenses and a new car.

It was to all parties concerned a twenty-four-karat investment in view of Williams's championship potential. There was, however, little time for A and B Boxing Enterprises to realize much profit from the venture. It was the following year that Williams met with his tragic accident.

Adams, upon hearing about the shooting, had Williams moved from Ben Taub into Methodist Hospital and summoned specialists to work on the fighter. Though convinced that Williams would never fight again, Adams felt an obligation to help him through the crisis, footing all the medical bills.

But "The Big Cat" was determined to fight again. Drawn, weak, and rail thin at less than one hundred and sixty pounds, he went to work on Hugh Benbow's cattle ranch near Yoakum, Texas. In this small town of six thousand, he put himself through a torturous routine of physical rehabilitation. He bailed hay and dug fence post holes to strengthen his body.

"That was a hard time for me," Williams admits. "And there were times when I was ready to give up. But I prayed to the Lord to give me the strength to keep going. I knew what I had to do—and that I needed his help to do it. I had to prove— to myself and a lot of other people—that I could come back, and I had some bills that had piled up. I wanted a new start, and the only way I saw to get it was to go back into the ring. So I kept on training."

Then, two years after his brush with death, he accomplished the first of his goals when he stepped into the ring in Houston to face opponent Ben Black. Following a ten-minute ovation from the crowd, he proceeded to knock out Black in the first round.

In quick succession, he won three additional bouts against less than awesome opposition before signing for the fight that would fulfill his second ambition. Two years after signing that original contract for the postponed fight with Cassius Clay, Williams got a second chance. This time, though, his opponent was calling himself Muhammad Ali, and he was the reigning world champion.

The fight was held in the Astrodome in front of the largest crowd to date to see a prize fight indoors—35,460—and the kind of payday Williams had not dared even dream of during those days back in the pulp mills. There was also the chance that he might, just might, dethrone the talkative Ali. Few knew that, just days before the big fight, Williams had suffered a sprained left thumb that was swollen and painful.

The bout was no contest. Ali, just twenty-four and in his prime, dominated his thirty-three-year-old challenger, smothering him with a barrage of punches. Even the pro-Williams crowd were yelling for referee Harry Kessler to stop the fight. By the time Kessler did declare Ali the winner in the third round, Wil-

liams's face was badly bruised. One eye was swollen shut, and
there was a cut on his lip that required five stitches to close.

Williams's cut of the record gate was in the neighborhood
of $100,000, but after lengthy legal bickerings, taxes, cuts, and
payments of debts, he finally received a check for only $7,471.

As far as the boxing world was concerned, Cleveland Williams was through. It appeared that the sport, so well known
for tossing over-the-hill and used-up boxers into the human trash
heap, had done the same to "The Cat." The road he had traveled
had been filled with more confusing turns and rough spots than
a man deserves and had now apparently reached a dead end.

For a while, he returned to work with old friend Viscusi,
serving as a sparring partner for some of the men who held
spots in the rankings he once owned. Occasionally, he fought
some up-and-comer or some big name on the way down, still
holding on for one more payday. The payoffs weren't big, neither
were the headlines.

Neither bothered Williams. He was, finally, a man at peace
with himself.

"You know," he says, "if I was fourteen years old again,
I'd probably do a lot of things the same way. Yeah, I'd probably
box. But what I would do differently is set out from the beginning
to find the best way to serve God and do it.

"If people would look at the things that happened to me
and listen to my story, they would understand what I'm talking
about. I'm lucky. Boxing didn't turn me into a bum. I didn't
let it. I managed to survive the hard times and live to get my
life in order. That's the answer, really. You've got to get your
life in order. Faith in the Lord is the most important thing a
man can have. It just takes some people a while to come to
that realization. Everybody's got to find it out for himself.

"God gave me the strength to sort out my life and look
at those things that are really important. A lot of things that
happened to me when I was younger really aren't important
anymore."

Today, at age fifty-two, Cleveland Williams weighs 225
pounds, barely over the weight he carried into the ring in the
Astrodome that night long ago when he faced Muhammad Ali.
He and his wife, Earnestine, have been happily married for seven

years. He has four children who demand a great amount of his time.

His children are still too young to know much about their father's background: how there was a time, ever so brief, when he was the toast of the boxing world. They don't know that he was once known as "The Big Cat"—a man who some said could have been the champion and was written up in *Time* and *Newsweek* and *Sports Illustrated*.

Cleveland Williams, now making a comfortable living for himself and his family as a truck driver, isn't a man locked in the past. There are no scrapbooks and precious few trophies of days gone by. Occasionally, he'll attend a fight, but not often. The sport, he says, isn't that exciting anymore—not like the old days. He'd rather spend a weekend with his wife and kids, fishing for bass or catfish.

Some say it's a shame that he didn't earn the kind of money that his talents promised, that it isn't fair that he should have to make those long hauls across the country, driving an eighteen-wheeler. Somehow, they say, Cleveland Williams deserved more.

"I know some people say that," he says. "I used to hear it a lot. But I never really listened. Because I've never felt short-changed. In fact, I consider myself very fortunate. I've got a good job, a good wife, and a good family. People looking for some guy to do a 'didn't boxing treat him bad' kind of story about don't need to waste their time talking to me."

When Williams went into the hospital last January for leg surgery to correct some blood flow problems from the unfortunate shooting so many years ago, children from his neighborhood flocked to see him. They aren't the kids Cleveland Williams has taught to box or entertained with stories of his athletic accomplishments. They are the kids he's talked to and counseled, urging them to make something of themselves and live Christian lives. Cleveland Williams isn't their hero, he's their friend.

"God's been good to me," he says. "He gave me a talent that I was able to use when I was young, and I used it as best I knew how at the time. I know there are people who look at boxing as something no Christian could ever justify. But I never had any problems with that. It was something I did—and I did it as fairly and as well as I could. I never tried to hurt anybody just for the sake of hurting them. Still, I gave boxing the best

I had. I always thought I owed that to myself and to the sport.

"I'm not one who looks back and does a lot of second-guessing. It's all behind me now and I'm comfortable with that fact.

"I've got a good life. The Lord has blessed me. In the long run, that's worth more than any championship belt or any amount of money a man can have in the bank."

Kyle Rote, Jr.

Soccer

IT WAS ONE OF THOSE sudden, eye-opening turn of events that so quickly restores lost perspective. It was 1974 and Kyle Rote, Jr., one of the nation's most celebrated young athletes, had been named the North American Soccer League's Rookie of the Year. He had also won the league scoring title that season

and added considerably to his reputation—and bank account—
by winning the ABC-TV Superstars Competition over some of
the most celebrated professional athletes in the country.

The same year, Betty Rote, Kyle's mother, suffered a cerebral aneurysm. The effects were similar to those caused by a
severe stroke. Suddenly, all the plaques and paychecks, the publicity and acclaim that had been focused on Kyle Rote meant little.
The woman who had been giving his life direction since he was
a young boy, who had provided him inspiration and encouragement, and who had always impressed him with her indomitable
Christian spirit was suddenly turning to him for explanations.

Her spirit broken, she could not understand why God had
singled her out, forcing this affliction on her. For the first time
in his life, Kyle found himself in the position of trying to lift
his mother's spirits, to lend her strength. "It was a strange situation," he remembers, "because all of my life she had been the
one providing me with strength and lifting me out of whatever
depressions I might have been dealing with. All I could tell her
was that I trusted God and knew that things happen for a reason.
I tried to assure her that God loved her and that I loved her.
But, honestly, I didn't feel that I was providing her the help
she so badly needed."

Why, he wondered, had it always been so easy for her to
help him? Betty Rote, a gifted speech therapist, had always
seemed to have the right solutions to his problems. Why wasn't
he able to find the words that would give her proper comfort
in her time of need?

Kyle remembers a time when he was sixteen years old and
had won the job of starting quarterback for Highland Park High
School in Dallas. The son of Pro-Football Hall of Fame standout
Kyle Rote, Sr., he was anxious to show the world that he, too,
would make his mark. In that season opener, Highland Park
was an overwhelming favorite as it prepared to face Fort Worth's
Paschal High. That evening, however, Kyle, Jr., threw two crucial
interceptions and fumbled twice as his team lost.

He returned home distraught and went straight to his room.
Lying on his bed, hidden by the dark, he replayed the game in
his mind. He had been terrible. He was embarrassed, discouraged,
and angry. A gentle knock came at his door. Betty Rote entered
and sat on the side of his bed, saying nothing for some time.

"Mom," Kyle finally said, "it was all my fault that we lost the game. I was awful."

She smiled and shook her head. "I think you've forgotten something," she said.

"Remember last summer when you came home from Young Life camp and told me how the atmosphere there—the sharing and the prayer—had helped you form a closer relationship with Jesus? You told me then that you realized sports wasn't the most important thing in the world, that God will love you regardless of whether you're a good athlete or not. Remember?

"If you'll think about it," she continued, "I believe you'll realize that something good may come from this defeat. Just give it a chance."

Indeed, something good did result from that opening night failure. Kyle Rote, Jr., recognized that overconfidence and too much personal pride can stand in the way of achieving real success. By the season's end, he was ranked among the best high-school quarterbacks in the nation, earning a spot on several high-school All-America teams.

"That's the way my mother always helped me," he says today. "She could put things into perspective with just a few words, a quiet suggestion, or even a certain look. It seemed so easy for her."

She had helped him through the confusion and hurt he had felt when she and his father had divorced. His mother explained that both his parents still loved him deeply and that he should not let their differences interfere with the feelings he had for his father and her. And when Kyle was in college and reached the decision that he no longer wanted to play football, she was immediately supportive.

He liked soccer, Kyle told her. He felt he might one day be good enough to play the game professionally and wanted to devote his full attention to it.

"Then that's what you should do," Betty Rote had told her son.

Outside of a modest number of Americans who were taking an interest in the sport, which enjoys fanatical popularity in one hundred and forty countries throughout the world, even the best of the North American Soccer League players were hardly celebrities. Even though Kyle Rote, Jr., had become the first native American to lead all NASL scorers (with ten goals and ten assists in the 1974 season), no manufacturers rushed to seek his endorsement on their products. No movie directors offered cameo parts to the twenty-three-year-old center forward, a bubble-gum card bearing his picture was not to be found, and Johnny Carson had not bothered to call. In fact, his first year salary of only $1,400 would have caused minor league baseball players, NBA benchwarmers, and pro-football rookies to even question his status as a professional athlete.

Then, however, came a call from the promotion department of ABC-TV inviting soccer's newest star to join a collection of the nation's professional athletes and compete in a decathlon-type event called the Superstars Competition. Designed as a television showcase of great athletes, its purpose was to lure a large number of the country's sports fans to sit and watch as men—such as NFL Player of the Year O. J. Simpson, Boston Celtics All-Pro John Havlicek, baseball's Pete Rose, hockey's Stan Mikita, tennis player Stan Smith, and auto racer Peter Revson—did battle in a ten-event program.

In all, forty-eight participants were asked to compete in four qualifying rounds, with the top twelve advancing to the two-day grand finale which would be shown on national television. To round out the field and add the spice of a possible darkhorse entry, ABC decided to invite representatives from stepchild sports, such as speedskating, track and field, and soccer. It was decided that the six-foot, 180-pound Rote could best represent the North American Soccer League.

Few gave him a chance to challenge seriously the big names of American sports. Yet, Kyle Rote, Jr., needed no prolonged thought to accept the invitation and immediately set about to prepare himself for the unique competition.

On the program would be ten events—100-yard dash, 880-yard run, 100-meter swim, tennis, baseball hitting, weightlifting, golf, bowling, a one-mile cycle race, and an obstacle-course run. Each competitor would choose seven events in which to compete but would be prohibited from choosing an event that coincided with the sport in which he earned his living. For instance, baseball star Reggie Jackson would not be allowed to compete in the baseball hitting, and, of course, Stan Smith would be barred from the tennis competition. A complex point system, giving ten points for first, seven for second, and so on, would eventually determine the overall winner.

Rote set about to prepare himself in a manner some would call obsessive. No sooner had the invitation been extended to him, he decided he would take full advantage of the opportunity given him. "The idea of being able to compete against some of the greatest athletes in the world," he told his wife, Mary Lynne, "is an exciting challenge. If I can do well, it could help to focus some attention on professional soccer. And we both know the money would come in handy." To a young bride attempting to set up housekeeping on a pro-soccer player's salary, the thousands of dollars being offered the winner of the Superstars Competition looked like a pot of gold at the end of a rainbow.

For eight back-breaking weeks, Kyle trained for the first round of the competition. He had not even owned a tennis racket, but he soon got one and was taking lessons at the famed T-Bar-N Tennis Club. He rented a couple of bicycles, and he and Mary Lynne decided to forego any other form of transportation for the weeks to come, riding to the store, to visit friends, and to classes where Kyle was completing his first semester at Perkins School of Theology in Dallas.

He joined the YMCA and worked out daily in the pool, strengthening himself for the 100-meter swim event. At a nearby bowling alley, he bowled over one hundred games. A friend who was a golf pro at a Dallas country club volunteered to give lessons to Kyle, whose only equipment was a starter set of clubs his parents had given him when he was twelve years old.

Always one to set high goals for himself, Kyle Rote, Jr., went quietly and feverishly about the task of transforming himself into an all-around athlete. The work paid off when he won the first round of competition, beating better-known athletes such as tennis great Rod Laver and baseball standouts Reggie Jackson and Jim Palmer.

At the mid-February finals in Rotondo, Florida, Rote wasted little time in making his presence known. On the opening day of competition, he defeated O. J. Simpson, John Havlicek, and basketball standout Jim McMillan to finish first in the tennis. That accomplished, he rushed out to the golf course and shot a respectable forty-three for nine holes. His score was good enough for second behind the forty-one score posted by Miami Dolphins safety Dick Anderson and better than the efforts of Pittsburgh Steelers running back Franco Harris, Pete Rose, and Stan Smith.

Later in the afternoon, facing defending Superstars champion Bob Seagren, the Olympic pole vaulter, the determined young soccer player scored an arm's length victory in the 100-meter swim. Later that evening, tired but eager to improve his total points, he defeated shot putter Brian Oldfield by forty-eight pins to take first place in bowling.

With four events behind him, Rote held a commanding lead. He was suddenly signing as many autographs and granting more interviews than the well-known athletes he was competing against.

On the second day, Kyle failed to place in the baseball hitting, an event he had won in the qualifying round, and was next to last in the grueling 880-yard run. But, in the cycle race, he finished a strong second to Dutch speed skater Ard Schenk. For the seven events in which he had chosen to participate, Rote had amassed forty-four points. His closest challenger, Seagren, accumulated thirty-eight.

For his efforts, Kyle Rote, Jr., received a check for $53,000 and a trophy signifying him as the Superstar of the Year. Suddenly, he was no longer just another face in the crowded world of professional sports.

In the span of the nationally televised event, the sports-crazed American public had found itself a new hero—a boyish-looking young man who ranked as something of a throwback to the all-but-forgotten Jack Armstrong days. Here was an almost shy divinity student soundly defeating high-salaried, well-publicized competitors from a pro-sports world, where the swinging lifestyle is commonplace and a million-dollar salary is life's brass ring.

In the aftermath of his victory, he told reporters that having been able to compete against athletes whom he had heard so much and read so much about for most of his life was one of the greatest thrills he had ever experienced. And what, they had wanted to know, was he going to do with his new-found wealth? "Life had been good to me," he explained, "so I have no intention of keeping all the money. I plan to share it with people who need it. To be honest, I've never worried much about having a lot of money."

With this, he packed his trophy and headed back to Dallas to the $85-a-month apartment he and his wife called home.

Rote's athletic career began as one might expect of a youngster with a famous football-playing father. It had been on the campus of Southern Methodist University, just a few blocks from the Rote home, where Kyle, Sr., had earned All-America honors.

Everyone felt that Kyle, Jr., was destined to follow in his dad's footsteps. As a senior at Highland Park—a school whose football tradition is dotted with names of alumni such as Doak Walker and Bobby Layne, NFL Hall of Famers—Kyle Rote, Jr., was the team's leader, an All-State quarterback and a defensive safety in his senior year. No fewer than fifty colleges offered scholarships to the gifted youngster, who had also captained the basketball and baseball teams.

And as a teenager, his goals weren't much different from those of most high-school athletes in Texas. "One day," he had said, "I would like to be good enough to play professional football. This is the goal I set for myself back when I first started playing."

Kyle carried this goal on to Oklahoma State University with him where his football career was short-circuited after only two months as a collegian. During a freshman team workout, he suffered a broken leg.

As he worked to rehabilitate the leg, isolated from the daily competition of workouts and games, young Rote began to take stock of his life. The atmosphere of big-time college athletics, he found, was not designed to help a struggling freshman—with less than ideal study habits—along the road to academic success. The athletes were housed in their own dorm, separated from the rest of the campus. Kyle began to question the course he had chosen for himself.

And, with time on his hands, he found himself thinking back to the summers before when, in an effort to keep himself in condition, he had joined some of his friends in games of sandlot soccer back in Dallas. The more he played the game and learned about it, the more he liked it. Soccer offered a challenge he could not totally understand or explain. All he knew was that he liked it and wanted to play more of it.

"I had so much fun playing soccer," he says, "that I wanted to become more involved in it. And it occurred to me that I was missing out on a lot of other things, being so involved in football and little else in college. I knew I didn't have the self-discipline to study the way I should with all the activity that goes on in a college dorm. In that kind of atmosphere, it takes a very dedicated person to keep his priorities in the proper order."

Thus, at the end of his freshman year, he transferred to the University of the South at Sewanee, Tennessee, giving up a full athletic scholarship to pay his own way. He spent his energies on his studies and his leisure time joining other nonscholarship athletes on the school's soccer team.

"A lot of people think it a little strange," Kyle says, "but my dad had as much to do with my decision to transfer as anyone. When I was growing up, he had frequently made it clear that he always needed an escape from football. We had a cottage on Long Island when we lived in New York, and he enjoyed going there to write poetry and paint. He was always telling me how important it was to have a vocation outside of football because football might not last that long. He made me aware that there were other things more important than sports.

"Actually, I did miss football for a while after I transferred; but as time went along, I just found soccer to be more enjoyable."

Rote switched his major from engineering to psychology, enjoyed a variety of campus activities, and, the day after his 1972 graduation, married a pretty sophomore from Georgia named Mary Lynne Lykins in the Sewanee chapel.

Another event transpired during the whirlwind days of his final spring at the university that would alter his life considerably. Rote was casually aware of the North American Soccer League. The formation of this league was an attempt to add yet another sport to the nation's professional sports menu. With teams composed almost entirely of transplanted European soccer players, the league had, in one form or another, been in existence since 1967. But it had received only a mild reception from the public and media alike.

Rote, then, was surprised to learn that the Dallas Tornado—the franchise in his hometown, which was owned by millionaire Lamar Hunt—had selected him as its number one draft choice that year. "I was tickled to death about it," Rote recalls. "But, to be quite honest, I wasn't even aware that they had a draft until I was selected."

The newlyweds returned to Dallas, set up housekeeping in a small apartment, and Rote began the pursuit of yet another athletic goal: that of being a professional soccer player. It was widely felt that Dallas's purpose in drafting the young Sewanee graduate was based more on publicity and promotional promise than in the player's abilities to compete with veterans from abroad who had played the game all their lives.

"The first time I saw him," recalls former Tornado coach Ron Newman, "he didn't look too polished. He was big and strong and eager to learn. But aside from those qualities, there wasn't too much to indicate that he was going to become one of the league's top players."

Rote was aware of the critical eye with which his every move as a professional was watched. He sought help and advice from his teammates and spent long hours on the practice field after other members of the Tornado had retreated to the showers.

His home debut came in Texas Stadium against the Toronto Metros in front of a crowd of 19,342, despite a day-long deluge. Rote did not disappoint them. In a 2–1 victory, he headed home the first goal, and it was his intimidating presence that helped set up the winning goal scored by teammate John Collins.

Clearly, Kyle Rote, Jr., was going to make a place for himself in pro soccer.

To do so, he worked hard. When he wasn't practicing on the field, he was seeking the help of his new bride at home. Mary Lynne would throw balls at him from various angles and shag for him in a nearby city park. "Kyle," she says, "has always been such a fierce competitor. He hates to lose at anything. I've never known anyone who works as hard as he does at whatever he sets his mind to do."

From that day forth, his life was a whirl of public appearances, recognition, and steady improvement as a soccer player. In his first season, the Tornado advanced to the NASL championship final before losing to Philadelphia. Twice during his playing career, Dallas won divisional titles.

And even as his excellence as a soccer player was gradually recognized, it was the annual Superstars competition that earned him his greatest athletic recognition. Following his initial victory in 1974, he won the title again in 1976 and 1977.

And along the way, he never overlooked an opportunity to talk with young people. "Throughout my playing career," he says, "I prayed every night that the inroads I was making would be used to a good purpose."

When he first entered the Perkins School of Theology, Rote's goal was eventual ordination as an Episcopalian priest. But soccer success and Superstars triumphs, he realized, provided him a broader, more wide-ranging base from which to share his convictions.

"Soccer," he says, "has literally millions of youngsters involved. It began to occur to me, even when I was playing, that I might have a greater influence, might better serve the Lord, if I didn't put on a clerical collar. Sports has provided me an opportunity to communicate with people—especially young people. Few get an opportunity to do this. I've always looked at what someone like Vince Lombardi did. As far as spiritual influence goes, he had as great an impact on the people he was involved with when he was coaching the Green Bay Packers as did the priest down the block."

Rote has carried his Christian message beyond his playing days. The sport of soccer, he has determined, is the platform he will use to carry the message of God's love.

When the Major Indoor Soccer League came into being, Rote was hired by the Memphis Americans to serve as vice-president for marketing and public relations. In essence, the new sport wanted Rote as its ambassador of goodwill. In 1983, he became general manager of the team and eventually coached the team until the franchise moved west prior to the 1984–85 season.

Today, he has again followed in his father's footsteps, working as a color commentator for television broadcasts of indoor soccer games. He's also done color on college football and recently began serving as an agent for several pro-soccer players. And he continues to speak at numerous Christian youth rallies throughout the country.

Kyle Rote, Jr., is still communicating with people. "I can't imagine myself not being involved in soccer and with people," he says. "In a sense, I have a debt to pay. Sports has been good to me. And it can be good to a lot of other youngsters. My job is to show them this."

Now, though, he is no longer talking of soccer. Rather, he is again reflecting on that trying time in 1974 when his mother was dealing with the problems brought on by her cerebral aneurysm.

"I prayed so hard for some guidance," he said. "I wanted so badly to be able to comfort her, to reassure her that things would be okay. But I just didn't feel I was doing everything for her that I could."

After five long months of hospitalization, Betty Rote was released and moved to San Antonio where she had a number of longstanding friends. She lived in a nursing home where she could get the daily attention and treatment she needed.

Being partially paralyzed and confined to a wheelchair was difficult for her to deal with at first. Kyle called her regularly and each time would hang up the phone with an aching heart. After a few weeks, however, this changed as he paid his first visit to his mother in her new residence.

"As soon as I entered the nursing home," he remembers, "I saw Mom in her wheelchair, talking with two patients who, I later learned, had suffered strokes. Mom wasn't just talking with them, she was giving them speech therapy, just as she had been trained to do. I watched the expressions on the people's faces as she talked with them and immediately knew she was back to the business of helping others. And it warmed my heart."

Betty Rote told her son, "I've found that I can help these people. I have something to give to them. Maybe that's why I'm here. Maybe that's the reason you told me to search for."

Kyle Rote, Jr., smiled and kissed her. His mother was still teaching him lessons about Christian faith and how it not only applies to life's joys, but its setbacks as well.

Johnny Robinson

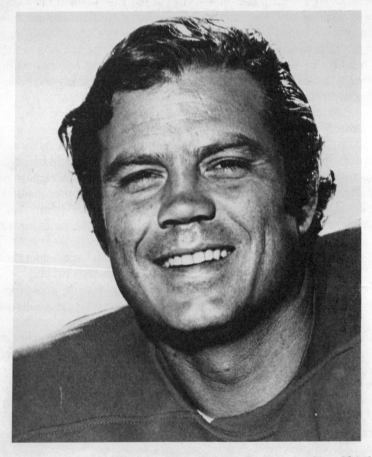

Former Defensive Back, Kansas City Chiefs

THE HAMBURGER, WHICH HAD been prepared for him an hour earlier, sat on the edge of his office desk, cold and untouched. There had been an endless series of phone calls to interrupt him and a myriad of minor problems that needed his attention.

Two youngsters were requesting money for haircuts, and another had stopped in to present him with a Father's Day card. There was a problem with some repair work on a second-hand bicycle and adult expertise was badly needed. Another youngster came to plead his case for no longer being grounded and for permission to attend a softball game that was scheduled later in the afternoon. And a basketball game was about to get underway in the backyard. Did he want to play?

It was—for all practical purposes—a typical lunch hour for Johnny Robinson.

For the former Kansas City Chiefs All-Pro defensive back, there are not enough hours in a day that begins at six in the morning and ends near midnight. On this particular Saturday, he was being pulled in a dozen different directions. He is the focus of attention of virtually all fourteen youngsters who reside at the Johnny Robinson Youth Home in Monroe, Louisiana.

Johnny Robinson is light years removed from the days when he starred in the Louisiana State University backfield and experienced the joys of a national collegiate championship. Years since his Super Bowl success with the Chiefs, Robinson is today carrying on a battle he considers far more important and demanding than any he ever experienced as an athlete.

Though an ordained minister in the World Ministry Fellowship, he no longer labors from the pulpit. Instead, he works with troubled youngsters in the shelter of an eighty-year-old mansion that sits on a picturesque two-acre plot in the older section of Monroe. There, he makes a home for boys aged nine to fourteen, who have had difficulties with the law and their previous home lives. His "children"—who all refer to him as "Dad"— have been arrested for theft and drug violations; they have been abused, mentally and physically; and they have experienced frightening academic difficulties. Almost without exception, they are kids whose lives were going nowhere in a galloping hurry.

Until they met Johnny Robinson.

Yet, few are impressed with the souvenirs from his football glory days which hang in his office. "These kids don't care in the least that I played pro ball or was on a Super Bowl winning team," he says. "In fact, if I were to tell them that someone like Joe Montana [San Francisco Forty-niners' quarterback] or

Tony Dorsett [Dallas Cowboys' running back] was coming here to speak to them, they wouldn't have the slightest idea who I was talking about. Generally, the kids we get here haven't had the benefit of the lessons that sports can provide. They're just not interested. They've been too busy trying to figure out how to survive."

For the former teammates who have lost touch with Johnny Robinson, it is no doubt difficult to picture the forty-five-year-old, one-time NFL standout in the role he now occupies. During those twelve years with the Chiefs, he enjoyed the reputation of one who lived life to the fullest, burned the candle at both ends, and loved every minute of it. When practice was over, he hurried to the welcome respite provided by neon night life and the challenges of business world success. Baton Rouge-born Johnny Robinson, son of a deacon in the Baptist church, loved the good life and pursued it with the same intensity with which he chased wide receivers on Sunday afternoons.

Before his retirement in 1972, Robinson was ranked as one of pro football's most prolific pass interceptors and one of its most wheeling-dealing businessmen. He owned a nightclub, a restaurant, and a racquet club. He was one of the beautiful people, wining, dining, and looking at life as one never-ending party.

Even when his playing days were over, Robinson held onto the game that had earned him fame and fortune. He served briefly as an assistant coach for the Jacksonville franchise of the short-lived World Football League, scouted for Hank Stram until he was fired as head coach of the Chiefs, then applied for and was awarded an assistant coaching position at Northeast Louisiana State in Monroe.

If there seems to be an indication of a downward spiral in those postplaying days moves, it is because they serve as valid examples of the personal difficulties Robinson was experiencing at the time. There was a divorce, some business failures, and a near-crippling battle with rheumatoid arthritis of the spine. And, as his physical condition worsened to a point where he was forced to walk with a cane and could no longer coach, Robinson seemed well on his way to becoming one of pro football's tragic stories.

Such, he insists, was never the case. A new faith in God, born during his coaching tenure in Jacksonville, saw him through the crisis period of his life.

Robinson had grown up in a strong Christian environment, but he carried on a determined youthful rebellion against the formalities of religion. Once away from home, enjoying the new-found freedom college life affords, he quickly drifted away from the church.

"I always thought of myself as a Christian," Johnny says, "but I wasn't working very hard at it—didn't for a number of years. But, then, while I was coaching in Jacksonville, I became acquainted with a lady who ran a bookstore that I frequented. She asked me one afternoon if I'd be interested in going to church with her some Sunday. I wasn't looking for any kind of a crutch at the time, you understand, but I went. And I got involved. Soon it dawned on me that my life had needs only the church could fill. This understanding really changed my whole life."

Even while coaching at Northeast Louisiana, he was ordained and began serving as a voluntary chaplain for the Monroe Police Department, ministering to prison inmates. Then, he became the associate pastor of a small Baptist church on the west side of town.

There are many who assume Robinson's enthusiastic return to the church was a result of his sudden recovery from the three-year bout with what had been diagnosed as an incurable arthritic condition. "I can't help but believe I had a divine sort of healing," he says, "because I simply woke up one day with no pain. And I haven't had any since. But my life has been touched in a number of other ways as well. No one miracle brought me to where I am today." It was his work as a jail minister that first brought to his attention the plight of many of the local children.

"I got a call one day from a teacher who asked me to visit a ten-year-old delinquent who had been arrested for stealing on several occasions. The kid had recently been returned to the state prison system. When I went out to see him, I found a tough but scared little boy who had been in trouble all his life. He had been abused by the other kids in the youth prison; and he related experiences I simply could not imagine any ten-year-old having gone through. I thought about the tremendous scars that were going to be left on his life. And as I drove back to town, I decided that I was going to see what I could do to help him and others like him. That ten-year-old kid helped me find my mission in life."

As he drove that day, he passed a stately old two-story home that sat on a lot occupying an entire block of South Grand Avenue in Monroe. There was a "For Sale" sign out front. The mansion would provide an ideal base for a home where youngsters, like the one he'd just met, might begin to rebuild their lives.

Johnny discussed the idea with his new wife, Cathy. He carefully explained his yet undeveloped plan for a youth home where children could grow up in a family atmosphere. "We had only been married for a short while," he says, "and what I was asking was something that would require a big commitment from her. There was no way I was going to be able to do it without her help. Fortunately, she embraced the idea immediately."

In time, the purchase of the house was completed. The Robinsons moved in, bought second-hand beds, had some extra bathrooms added, enlarged the dining room, and prepared for the new challenge. Impatient, Johnny went to a local judge and had the aforementioned ten-year-old released to him even before the Johnny Robinson Youth Home was officially open.

This was in 1979, several hard-time years ago.

"At the start," he admits, "I was very idealistic about the whole thing. I thought I could run the home on private donations and the money I'd set back from my playing days. I saw the place running like something out of an old Bing Crosby movie. People would bring homeless kids to us, we'd love them and care for them, and everything would be great."

Clearly, he did not anticipate the financial hardships that soon followed. As the population of the Johnny Robinson Youth Home grew, so did the money problems. At one point, he was forced to sell the family car to make the monthly mortgage payment on the house.

"I got to a point," he laughs, "where the only transportation I had was a used riding lawnmower. I drove it to and from the store to buy groceries."

But, with food bills that ran $3,000 a month and utilities costing $1,000, Robinson was struggling. It became more and more difficult to afford the second-hand bicycles that he traditionally gave to each new resident upon his arrival or to come up with the five dollar bill he awarded each report card A that was brought home.

Robinson quickly admits that he was, and is, a less than polished fund-raiser. He refuses, for instance, to accept pay for speaking engagements in a time when many of today's religious leaders and Christian athletes command $1,500 fees for their public testimony. "Oh, I'm not hesitant to talk to the Jaycees or someone and ask if they can help us with a few bicycles or a new lawnmower," he says. "But I have a hard time asking outright for financial donations."

Without his asking, however, many of his former LSU teammates have responded to his needs, providing considerable financial help, particularly in the struggling early days of the home's existence. And some of his Kansas City teammates have lent a hand.

"I went back to Kansas City for a team reunion a few years ago," Johnny says, "and stayed with [defensive tackle] Ed Lothamer. He asked what we needed at the home and I told him I was looking around for a good used van to carry the kids to the lake and ball games and places like that. After I got back to Monroe, a dealer in town called me and said that Ed had called and arranged to buy one for us. And [former Chiefs quarterback] Lenny Dawson has helped out a good deal."

The major struggles are now history for the five-year-old operation. Now licensed by the state of Louisiana, it receives state funding along with private donations, which last year amounted to $23,000. But the Robinsons are not on Easy Street. It is necessary to purchase food wholesale to remain within the strict budget Robinson has set. And the number of residents has grown from two to fourteen over the years. Today, Johnny and Cathy have the help of a part-time tutor, a social worker, and three college students who assist with the running of the home.

For the more than forty youngsters who have spent time there, little has changed. On a table in Robinson's office there is the same fruit bowl that greeted the first residents, filled with apples, oranges, and bananas.

"I tell the boys they can eat all they want," he says. "It's funny to watch the newer kids. They'll come in and eat a half dozen bananas at one sitting. It's like they're afraid it might be their last chance, so they're going to get as much as they can. It's just not something they're used to at first."

Nor are they used to the love and concern that pours forth

from "Mom" and "Dad" Robinson. Cathy has devised a color-coded clothes hamper system to enable each youngster to keep track of his own clothes on wash day. (Wash day is *every* day and has caused three washers and dryers to go by the wayside thus far!) Cathy also supervises the cooking.

"The only problem I've had with the entire thing," Mrs. Robinson says, "is trying to figure out where in the world all the missing socks go. I've got a huge plastic bag filled with socks that have no mates. I've told Johnny on a number of occasions that I'll never consider this operation a complete success until I find where all those other socks have gone."

Others, however, are ready to judge the Johnny Robinson Youth Home a roaring success, missing socks and all. Youngsters who have come under Robinson's supervision have shown marked improvement academically, socially, and physically. "We've had some failures," he says, "but we've had some successes, too.

"For me, it has been the most rewarding experience of my life, far more so than national championships or Super Bowls. I guess in a way it's like playing the Super Bowl every day, only with lives at stake instead of a ring and a big payday.

"What we're trying to do here is to provide a family environment for these kids. Quite honestly, we're in the problem business, trying to resolve things having to do with family, education, and self-worth. But our role is minor, really. The only thing that can change a child's heart is the Lord. If they can come to that understanding, with our help, they're on the right track. I do a good deal of praying with the kids and try to explain to them the purpose of prayer."

On Sundays, Robinson conducts an informal home service for those who do not choose to attend local churches in Monroe. "We keep our religion pretty simple, basic," he says. "But we emphasize its importance. Without it as a foundation, we'd never have been able to make it. I try, as best I can, to make the kids aware of that."

He smiled and dealt with another problem brought him by a youngster who suggested there was some cheating going on in the basketball game outside. Johnny Robinson hugged the boy, rose, and said he was going to come play—and there had better be no rule violations while he was on the court.

On his desk, the hamburger remained, untouched.

Scott Appleton

All-American Tackle

IT WAS ONE OF THOSE crisp, sunny January days of which college bowl game promoters dream. The matchup was scheduled to take place in the historic Cotton Bowl in Dallas before a sellout crowd of seventy-six thousand and a national television audience.

The 1964 Cotton Bowl would be played for the highest prize that college football has to offer—the national championship. The University of Texas—unbeaten and one of the country's finest defensive units—was ranked number one in both the Associated Press and United Press International polls. Its opponent, Navy—with strong-armed, scrambling quarterback Roger Staubach directing an outstanding offense—was ranked number two. Both coaches, Navy's outspoken Wayne Hardin and Texas's homespun Darrell Royal, were admitting that the championship spoils should indeed go to the victor.

Most experts predicted that the game's outcome would be decided by Staubach's success or failure against the Longhorns' defense. Owner of the Heisman Trophy, Staubach had just been selected as a future draft selection by both the National Football League Dallas Cowboys and the American Football League Kansas City Chiefs. He was regarded as a game-breaker. If Texas was to slow him, much of the responsibility would fall on the sizable shoulders of All-American tackle Scott Appleton. A senior, Appleton had only recently been named winner of the prestigious Outland Trophy, which goes annually to college football's premier lineman.

Appleton's name would be heard often that afternoon. He repeatedly broke through the frustrated Navy offensive line to drop Staubach for a loss or force him to rush his passes. Despite the unrelenting pressure, Staubach established a Cotton Bowl passing record that day; but Appleton and his Longhorn teammates claimed the lion's share of the glory. They led 21–0 at halftime and then coasted to a 28–6 victory and claimed all of the national championship hardware that awaited.

"In all the years I played ball," says Staubach, who went on to professional stardom with the Dallas Cowboys, "I can't remember an afternoon when I was dealt more misery. Every time I looked up, Scott Appleton was in my face. It was almost as if he was lining up in our backfield."

The Cotton Bowl reviews were yet another jewel in the athletic crown of the big, easy-going kid from the Central Texas community of Brady. Since the days when Appleton was an All-State lineman for the Brady High Bulldogs, football stardom had come easy. He was good and he knew it. He knew it long before the endless stream of college recruiters came, trying to persuade him to attend their schools. He knew it long before he was officially recognized as a college All-American and before the Outland judges chose him to receive their distinguished award—long before he made life miserable for Roger Staubach in front of millions at the Cotton Bowl.

And Appleton was dead certain of his talent when the Houston Oilers came up with a $150,000 bonus. The bonus was to convince him that his professional football career would be better spent in the then-youthful AFL rather than the established NFL. The world, in a sense, was Scott Appleton's for the asking.

That's the way it was once—recognition, acclaim, money, a loving wife, a family, and several solid business opportunities. But they didn't last long. And Scott Appleton, unable to cope with disappointment and the first bitter tastes of failure, went from top to bottom.

Only now, several years after his athletic glories, is he making a comeback, rebuilding, taking a new and different look at life's priorities.

The 6'3", 245-pounder (whose trophy case once ran to overflowing) admits that he, like so many in his particular field, overdosed on fame, press clippings, money, and the good life. He was a cinch, members of the media repeatedly noted, to make it to superstardom as a professional. The logical progression from high school All-State to college All-American called for him to soon become an All-Pro performer with the Oilers.

Instead, Appleton found himself sitting on the bench, watching a losing team play Sunday after Sunday. He had gone from the Outland Trophy winner to being a seldom-used backup defensive lineman—from the national championship to membership on one of the league's doormats. Compounding the problem was the fact that many of the Oiler veterans made it all too clear they resented the high salary and bonus he received while contributing very little on game days.

Pressures built; and Appleton's attitude toward the game he had so long loved and enjoyed changed dramatically.

"By the time I got to the Oilers," he says, "I was totally convinced I was the greatest thing since sliced bread as far as football was concerned. I had come to expect people to treat me like I was something special. From that, I went to a very confusing situation as a professional. For the first time in my life, I began to experience exasperation, frustration, and great disappointment."

Thus, he began to drink heavily and pop amphetamines like Life Savers—five or so before a game, a couple before each practice. There were nights when it took a fifth of whiskey or a case of beer to bring him down from his "speed" high so he could sleep.

"When I was still in excellent shape, still playing, I could drink and stay up all night and still be ready to go at practice the next day. I could handle it—or so I thought."

After three dismal years with the Oilers, Appleton was traded to the San Diego Chargers. There, he enjoyed a brief career resurgence, playing well for a couple of seasons. But by then, other aspects of his life were beginning to shatter. His wife filed for divorce, and his financial advisors—eager to help him when he was still in the chips—left him when he went "worse than broke" in a fried chicken franchise business venture.

With each disappointment, the drinking increased. "It became a problem in every aspect of my life," he admits, "affecting everything. Before I realized what was happening, it was a very serious problem."

Scott himself was becoming a problem for the Chargers; and he was released just prior to the beginning of his third year in San Diego. "Frankly," he says, "I had become something of a discipline problem."

On top of everything else, football had become a painful chore for the man to whom it had always been so easy, so joyful. "When you get close to thirty," he says, "it all becomes something of an unnatural state—the violence and the physical demands. I lost my enthusiasm and knew it was time to think about getting out anyway. I was doing pretty well in the stock market at the time, so I figured it was time to pursue a more normal life."

He even sought help from Alcoholics Anonymous but experienced little success. "I just couldn't stop drinking. All I seemed to be accomplishing was making myself more and more miserable."

Maybe, he thought, a return to football would put some purpose, some spark back into his life. He thought that it might also provide financial salvation. Soon after he was released by the Chargers, the stock market bottomed out, dealing Appleton yet another overwhelming financial loss.

"I tried to get back into football," he says, "but I couldn't make it. I made a feeble attempt to catch on with the New Orleans Saints, but by then I was drinking so much I just couldn't get in the proper shape."

For the next six years, Scott Appleton was drunk. He remembers little about those times. "I just stayed bombed out," he says.

For two of those trying years, he was a stockbroker in Houston with only marginal success. For a couple of years, he lived at home in Brady, helping his father run a small ranch. Then he drifted to San Antonio to live with an uncle.

"My uncle told me he would give me a free apartment," Scott says, "and that he would help me get a new start. At the time, I was at the absolute bottom. I'll never forget arriving in San Antonio. I had sixty-three cents in my pocket."

The $150,000 "bonus baby" was on his last leg.

"One of the first things I did was go to a doctor to see if he could offer me some kind of treatment for my drinking. He checked me out and told me I was starting at the wrong place. He put me in touch with Dr. Jimmy Allen, minister of the First Baptist Church in San Antonio."

It was Dr. Allen who pointed Appleton in the direction of an upward course. "I met with Dr. Allen a couple of times a week, and, after about three months, I began to feel as if I was getting a grip on things. By the grace of God, I was set free of my craving for alcohol. With God's help, I began trying to put my life back together. The only way I could have done it was through a process of spiritual growth that eventually led me to accept Jesus Christ as my Savior. With Dr. Allen's help, I began to learn how to pray and to seek out the disciplines necessary for spiritual growth."

It is something Appleton has been working hard at ever since. There are challenges to being a Christian, he says, and goals to be reached. And he had dealt with both on a regular basis as an athlete.

"The problem in sports," he says, "is that you get carried so high. When you've got seventy thousand people sitting in the stands, cheering for you, it's an incredible high—everything afterwards is very anticlimatic. I read, for instance, where Dorothy Hamill, the figure skater, said she was miserable for a long time after winning the Olympic gold medal because she had no goal left in her life.

"I once had that same feeling, but that's changed. Now my goal is to help other people who are depressed and down on their luck."

But Scott Appleton is the first to admit he's far from home free in his own life struggle. "I'm resigned to the fact it is going to be a day-to-day battle for the rest of my life. I'm comfortable in that knowledge. What you have to do is get up every morning, looking forward to the battle.

"There's still this adversary voice inside that tells me I should go out and try to make a million dollars and regain all the fame and fortune that I lost. I've been a Christian now for seven years, but I'm still in the infancy stages of my Christianity. I still have my ups and downs. But, the ups aren't as high and the downs aren't nearly as low."

The ups, for that matter, far outnumber the downs.

After he was baptized in 1977, Appleton was offered a job managing the Fourth Street Inn, a San Antonio restaurant that is part of the First Baptist Church's downtown street ministry. The food is simple but plentiful; the clientele are the down-and-outers. The small profits from the inn help to support a free-food program and counseling service to those fighting problems with alcohol and drugs.

Scott considered the offer, but declined. He was not yet ready to quit chasing the big bucks brass ring. "Actually," he says, "I had not grown enough as a Christian."

In time, however, the job was offered him again—and Appleton took it. "I had grown some spiritually by then and felt a calling to take it. It finally sunk into me that I might be able to do somebody some good there.

"What we try to do with our street ministry is to show people that when doctors and psychiatrists and all efforts by other men fail, Christ can come into your life and take over. Hey, I'm a walking, talking billboard of the truth of that fact," he says.

In addition to his work with the street ministry restaurant, Appleton travels to speak at church gatherings, telling of his bout with alcoholism. "I tell people, young people mostly, about how you can be at the top of this world and then go to the bottom and still wind up finding something better—eternal life. It's peaceful and fulfilling, and it's forever."

Thus, the lifestyle of the former sports' world superstar has changed dramatically. There are no spotlights, no headlines, no autograph-seekers, or celestial bank accounts. His pay at the inn is nominal. The small apartment he calls home is most kindly referred to as modest. There are no trophies—except for the one his University of Texas teammates awarded him for being selected the team's "Most Outstanding Leader."

"That one," he says, "is the greatest award I ever received. I wish I had been mature enough at the time to realize its importance. Things might have been different. Who knows?"

Today's Scott Appleton is a man setting new goals.

"I'm still praying for guidance as to what to do," he says. "I want to start a Bible study class. And I'd like to get more involved in going into the schools to talk with kids. Maybe I can help a few of them avoid some of the wrong turns I took.

"And, I still think I've got the ability to make money—maybe a million. I've been thinking about getting into some kind of restaurant business. But I don't want to get so involved in money-making that I lose perspective. When you lose that, the next thing you know, you're back in the jungle. I've been there and, believe me, I don't want to try it again.

"In a sense, this is a whole new ball game for me, and, with the Lord's help, I'm playing to win. In sports, I always did. And I'm playing this game harder than any I've ever played."

Kevin Curnutt

A Real Winner

THE POLISHED TILE HALLWAY outside the Arlington Community Hospital emergency room quietly echoed the whispers of the doctor as he stood, grim-faced, trying to comfort the parents of the dying thirteen-year-old boy whom he had just examined. For Jerry and Gail Curnutt, the couple to whom he was speaking, the past few hours had dissolved into a sequence of bizarre events born of nightmares not reality. Suddenly, nothing made sense.

That January Sunday afternoon four years ago, so full of activities, so carefully planned, was not supposed to end in a strange hospital with a strange doctor talking of death.

The family had attended church services that morning, had lunch, and the elder Curnutts planned to spend the early part of the afternoon at the church, teaching country and western dance lessons to a group of junior-high students. The lessons would be cut shorter than usual, everyone had agreed, so they might get home in plenty of time to see the kickoff of the Super Bowl.

Kevin Curnutt, Jerry and Gail's youngest son, was visiting a friend nearby, riding motorcycles on some trails in a wooded pasture across from the south Arlington, Texas, church.

It was just minutes after 3 P.M., however, when a carefree day turned into a pitch black horror with which the family still lives. A sniper—a quiet mystery man who lived as a recluse near the property on which the youngsters were riding their dirt bikes—shot and killed fourteen-year-old Trey Shelton and seriously wounded Kevin Curnutt.

The only explanation the Arlington police had been able to come up with was that the noise from the motorbikes had upset the gunman.

"It's best," the doctor said, "if you don't go in to see him. We haven't had a chance to clean him up yet."

"Will he be okay?"

"I have to be honest with you," he said. "Your son is critically injured and unconscious. He won't know you are here."

The doctor went on to explain that Kevin had been shot in the head, a fragment from a twelve-gauge shotgun shell entering one side, traveling completely through his brain, and exiting on the other side. Chances were their son might not live more than another thirty minutes.

As she listened to the doctor talk, Gail Curnutt knelt down and, with a handkerchief she had been wadding into knots since the race to the emergency room, wiped her son's blood from one of the doctor's shoes.

"I think," she said as she stood, "that we should go in right away."

As afternoon crept to evening, then night, Jerry Curnutt paced the hospital corridors in a state of shock. It was, he says, as if his brain was overheated. "The only way I can describe my feeling is to say it was as if I had spent a lot of time looking directly into the sun," he says.

In his confused, desperate state, Jerry tried to form some reason for what had occurred just hours earlier. There had, he realized, been warning signs that such an insane tragedy might occur. Several months earlier, his son had returned home to tell him of "some old guy" who lived near the Sheltons chasing him and his friend Trey with a shovel. Jerry listened to the story, made certain the boys had not been on the man's property, then dismissed the incident. It was, he decided, a case of teenage exaggeration.

Then, later, there had been the overheard conversation between Kevin and Trey about a quarterhorse owned by Trey's father, former Arlington City Councilman Ralph Shelton, being killed by a shotgun blast on New Year's Eve. The Shelton youngster mentioned the $25,000 cutting horse had been found dead "down at the barn." Jerry Curnutt, who had never visited the Shelton home, had no idea the barn was on the same seventeen-acre plot where the family's residence was located.

Still, for someone—no matter how deranged his mind might be—to wait in hiding and shoot two defenseless youngsters was light years beyond his comprehension.

It was shortly after 10 P.M. when Jerry Curnutt passed a waiting room television set and heard a reporter giving details of the shooting. Both youngsters, the reporter was saying, had been killed.

Jerry, still not certain he wasn't trapped in some bad dream, turned and ran back to the intensive-care ward with tears in his eyes.

For the first time since his and Gail's arrival at the hospital, he felt a small rush of relief when he saw that his son, defying all odds the medical staff had given him, was still clinging to life.

Kevin Curnutt's and Trey Shelton's friendship had developed quickly after each had enrolled for the eighth grade at

Arlington's newly opened Floyd Gunn Junior High School in the fall of 1980. They shared several classes and were teammates on the football team. In short order, they were spending time in each other's homes, staying overnight, and occasionally taking trips with Trey's father to attend cutting horse competitions. Rare was the weekend they did not spend in each other's company.

The Saturday before the shooting, Trey had spent the night with Kevin. "I remember them being back in Kevin's room, laughing until late in the night," Gail Curnutt says. "In fact, I finally had to go in and tell them to quiet down and get to sleep because we were going to church the next morning."

Kevin and Trey were invited to attend the Sunday afternoon dance lessons but mentioned they were planning to go over to the Sheltons after lunch and ride dirt bikes.

Thus, the next day the Curnutts and another couple were busy with the dance instructions when an unknown man entered the back door of the church and spoke briefly with one of the other instructors. He, in turn, walked over to Jerry and informed him there might be a sniper in the woods across the street.

After advising all those in the church not to leave the building, Jerry Curnutt walked out onto the front steps and saw several police cars lined up along South Bowen Road. An ambulance and a paramedic team had also arrived. A police officer, seeing him standing on the church steps, yelled for him to "get back inside."

Panic tightened in his chest, and Jerry ran immediately to his car and drove it fifty yards to where the police officers were assembled. Parking near the ambulance, he took the little cover that a nearby telephone pole provided. He asked what had happened.

The paramedic told him that two boys had been shot, and a sniper was barricaded in the house across the street. One of the victims had been picked up and taken to the hospital. They had not yet been able to reach the body of the other.

Curnutt immediately drove back to the church to tell his wife what he had learned. Standing on the porch, the hectic police activity in full view, he repeated to her what the paramedic had said. Gail Curnutt, her mouth suddenly dry, listened, saying nothing. Then she fainted.

While others tended Gail, Jerry telephoned the Shelton

house. It was Trey's sister's birthday, he knew, and some sort of celebration had been planned. Trey's sister answered and said her mother was out walking with a neighbor. Curnutt briefly told her of the possible danger in the woods and advised her to remain in the house.

In just a matter of minutes, a call came to the church from the hospital, asking that the Curnutts get there as quickly as possible.

As they entered the emergency room, they saw Trey's mother, Roselin, talking with a plainclothes police officer. Jerry remembers hearing the officer ask if she was Mrs. Shelton, then telling her, "Your son is dead."

It was some time before the Curnutts learned the full details of the tragic event that brought them to Arlington Community Hospital on that cold, suddenly dreary, Sunday afternoon.

Only after talking with Arlington police investigators did they find out that their son had been ambushed by a man named Richard Wade Tiedemann, a thirty-two-year-old aerospace engineer employed by the Vought Corporation. For four years, Tiedemann had lived alone in the two-bedroom house adjacent to the Shelton property. Others in the neighborhood described him as a "loner" who rarely spoke to anyone and always kept the gate to his property locked. Born in Texas City, he had graduated with honors from the University of Virginia and earned a master's degree from Princeton. Tiedemann spent a great deal of his time raking leaves in his oak-shaded yard or working on the sailboat he had recently purchased. No one seemed to really know him.

A search of Tiedemann's house revealed that he also owned a number of guns. In fact, when he'd paid a Christmas visit to his parents' home in Texas City a month earlier, he had taken all his guns with him, explaining to his father that he was fearful someone might break into his house during his absence and steal them.

It was the previous November when Tiedemann had called the Arlington Police Department to complain about the excessive noise made by dirt bikes being ridden on the property next to his house. Police records indicated that an officer drove to the area and spoke to young Trey Shelton and several of his friends about the matter following Tiedemann's call. Neither the police nor Tiedemann ever spoke with Trey's parents about the complaint.

In truth, there was little the authorities could do since the bikes were being ridden on the Shelton property. It was also noted there had never been any complaint from anyone else living in the same neighborhood.

On that Sunday, however, Richard Tiedemann apparently decided to take the law into his own hands. He loaded his twelve-gauge shotgun, stepped over the barbed wire fence separating his property from the Sheltons, and positioned himself behind a concrete outbuilding. It was, according to the mother of a five-year-old boy who witnessed the shootings, approximately 3:30 P.M.

Tiedemann waited until young Shelton, riding ahead of the inexperienced Kevin (who had been riding his friend's bike for just a couple of weeks), topped a small rise on the dirt road running adjacent to the fence line. Two shots were fired, knocking Trey from his bike. Hit in the back and the head, he died almost immediately, according to the medical examiner.

The third shot was aimed at Kevin Curnutt and struck him in the head. He fell, and the red bike he'd been riding toppled over on him.

Tiedemann then rose from his kneeling position, his rifle at his side, and slowly walked back to his house without even looking back in the direction of his fallen victims.

Arlington detectives R. A. Puente and T. C. Ingram received word from dispatch of a call about a possible sniper shooting and were at the scene in a matter of minutes. They quickly determined the Shelton youngster appeared to be already dead. From their vantage point, they could see that Kevin Curnutt was convulsing and apparently was still alive.

As soon as the medical unit arrived, Ingram drove his police car through the gate to shield the ambulance attendants who made their way to Kevin and hurriedly returned him to the ambulance. Getting to Trey Shelton was impossible since the gunman was evidently still in the house and might start firing at any moment.

The Tactical Unit soon arrived and was in position while attempts were made to talk Tiedemann from the house. Once, as the surrounding officers waited, the suspect walked, almost casually, from the house to the garage. He stayed for a few minutes, then returned toward the front porch, the shotgun at his side. As he stepped up on the porch, he turned suddenly and fired in the direction of the officers. Several return shots were fired and Tiedemann screamed, reached for his leg, and fell. Obviously wounded, he crawled back into the house.

It was after six when tear gas cannisters were finally shot through the front window, and a small fire broke out. Shortly thereafter, Tiedemann lunged out the front door, fell to the ground, and again began shooting. Marksmen from the Tactical Unit returned fire, killing him.

Thus, Richard Tiedemann's explanation as to why he had lain in waiting and shot two teenage boys died with him.

For almost three weeks, Kevin lay in a coma. Despite a seemingly endless stream of relatives and friends coming to the hospital, the Curnutts rarely left their son's side. They did attend Trey Shelton's funeral and occasionally would make a quick trip home for clean clothing or to check the mail, but there was always a rush to get back to the hospital—back to Kevin.

Constantly, Jerry and Gail and their oldest son, Kelly, talked to Kevin. They told stories, read aloud, sang songs, and prayed prayers in hope they might be heard by the youngster who lay motionless.

One visiting doctor, who dropped in on Kevin and saw the determined, hopeful looks on the faces of the family members, stayed only briefly before stepping out into the hall and disappearing quickly around the corner. There he broke into tears. Even if the youngster lived, the doctor believed, he would be little more than a vegetable in whatever time remained for him. Though the swelling in Kevin's brain was still too severe to determine the full extent of the damage, doctors were already preparing the Curnutts for the worst.

As the days passed, the Curnutts were told of the disquieting list of possibilities to prepare for—paralysis, blindness, inability to speak, and loss of memory and all motor abilities. And, of course, there was a very real chance that Kevin might never awaken from his comatose state.

"We came to the point," says Mrs. Curnutt, "that we no longer let the negative opinions affect us. The doctors and nurses were simply trying to prepare us for the worst. We realized what they were doing. What they didn't seem to realize was that we were busy preparing for something entirely different."

For parents, who had gone so far as to sign organ donor agreement papers, the fact Kevin was still alive was as positive a sign as they needed.

But each day presented some new crisis. Following surgery, Kevin's temperature rose dramatically and refused to subside for several days. And there was no indication that he was responding to any of the stimulus provided him. The family continued to talk, to sing, to read—but there was no evidence Kevin was hearing them. Sadly, doctors and nurses were even more certain of their earlier diagnoses.

It was on a Sunday afternoon, three weeks after the shooting, that a nurse stood feeding Kevin small spoonfuls of ice cream. As she fed him, she, like Mrs. Curnutt, carried on a running stream of conversation with the patient. "I'll bet you're getting tired of this ice cream," she said. "What you probably would like is a big ol' pizza with everything on it."

Gail smiled and joined the conversation. The mention of pizza, she said, reminded her of the time Kevin and one of his friends had climbed through some playground-like cubicles designed for smaller, younger children in one of the pizza restaurants.

She went on to explain how he had gotten stuck while attempting to crawl through one of the small, gaily colored openings. The nurse, joining into the one-sided conversation, said to Kevin, "You must have really been a sight. Your rear end must have been a foot in the air!"

Suddenly, Kevin Curnutt was laughing. His mother laughed with him, then cried. It was, she says, a miracle.

No longer comatose, Kevin was transferred from the intensive-care unit to a private room the following day, his condition changed from critical to serious. Though still completely immobile, the youngster was alert and aware of those around him. His speech had not yet returned but, through the use of an alphabet board designed by his older brother, he was able to communicate on a limited basis. His greatest response came from the steady flow of tapes that were delivered from his former schoolmates who wished him a speedy recovery and kept him updated on what was happening at school.

"Seeing his eyes light up as he listened to those tapes sent by his friends," says his father, "was worth a million dollars."

Two weeks later, Kevin was transferred to the Baylor Medical Center for a battery of tests and physical therapy. After three more weeks, doctors told the Curnutts they could take their son home.

For eight years, Gail Curnutt had been working as an elementary school teacher. Her career, however, was set aside so that she might remain home, tending to the constant needs of her injured son.

Frustrations came quickly, in waves. She did everything she could to see that Kevin was comfortable, yet saw his condition worsening daily. For reasons over twenty doctors could not determine, Kevin could not keep food on his stomach. In time, even the mention of food caused him to become ill. He had weighed 155 pounds when he was shot and was down to 130 when he returned home from Baylor Hospital on June first.

A month later, his weight had dropped to 100 pounds. "He was at the point where he was going to die if something wasn't done," Jerry Curnutt says. "The doctors even called in a psychiatrist to determine if maybe Kevin was actually trying to kill himself."

Kevin was admitted to Arlington Memorial Hospital on July fourth and, for the next several weeks, was fed interveinously a mega-calorie liquid diet while doctors attempted to determine the problem. Eventually, it was discovered that he was suffering from hypercalcemia (an excessive amount of calcium in the blood), an ailment common to adolescent males who are immobile. Medication controlled the problem, and soon Kevin was again eating normally and regaining his weight.

But with the good news, it seemed, there was always the bad. A neurosurgeon reviewed the results of a brain scan he had done and told Jerry and Gail that there was little hope their son would ever be able to move. The injury had damaged the motor skills area of the brain.

On their doctors' advice, the Curnutts took Kevin to Denver for a two-month stay at the Craig Rehabilitation Hospital. There, the family went through an intensive training program on the care of quadraplegics. Gail stayed the entire two months, living in an apartment near the hospital.

While Kevin would miraculously be mentally sound and his speech and eyesight were not affected—there had been no nerve damage and he would retain his complete sense of feel—hope of walking or having use of his arms and hands was out of the question.

"The people telling us these things," remembers Jerry Curnutt, "were highly trained professionals for whom we had a great deal of respect. But we simply could not accept their conclusions. We had no idea when or how, but we felt strongly that the day would come when Kevin would be able to walk again. We just had to keep searching and praying that we might find the way."

In the meantime, they tried to provide their son with as normal a life as possible. One of the first orders of business was to solicit the services of a homebound teacher so that Kevin might continue with his education. The Curnutts had their van equipped with a lift and, strapped into a wheelchair, Kevin enjoyed occasional weekend outings for chicken fried steak and a movie with friends or his brother.

But, for almost a year, there was little, if any, sign of physical progress.

The following fall, Kelly Curnutt suffered a knee injury during football practice. Enroute to the doctor's office, Jerry Curnutt heard a news item on the car radio about an antigravity platform that had been created by NASA to help brain-damaged children learn to walk.

Jerry immediately began placing calls, trying to learn more information on the device. The local station directed him to the CBS offices in New York. They, in turn, put him in touch with NASA's Ames Research Center in Mountain View, California. A dozen or so calls later, Jerry was talking with a staff member of The Institute for the Achievement of Human Potential in Philadelphia, a facility specializing in the treatment and rehabilitation of brain-damaged children.

The next stop in the Curnutt odyssey was Philadelphia. It was there, finally, that they found the hope for which they'd long been searching.

"Kevin was ready to try something new," his mother says. "The Philadelphia institute offered us something encouraging.

They operate on the philosophy that a very small part of the brain does all the physical work for the body. If another part of the brain can be trained to take over the motor function of the damaged part, a reteaching process can result in messages being sent to the limbs."

Told there was a year-long waiting list, the Curnutts were insistent, repeatedly contacting the institute to ask if there had been any cancelations. In November of 1982, five months after their first contact, they were at the facility with Kevin. Tests were performed, and the Curnutts, including Kelly, spent five fourteen-hour days being instructed in the program and the procedures it involved.

The basis of the still controversial Philadelphia program is "patterning," which involves five people working together, moving the patient's body in a crawling motion. The concept, originated in the 1950s, is that repeated physical movements develop new motor pathways that signal the brain as to what is expected. Simply stated, the motions teach a new part of the brain to signal the motor skills to the body. The patient, just like an infant, must learn the motor functions from the beginning. First, he learns to crawl.

The Curnutts returned home to make arrangements to begin the program in their home. Their garage was converted into a bedroom/therapy room and, with the help of his father, Jerry Curnutt began to build the necessary equipment (designed by the institute) for the patterning procedure.

Operating on an out-patient format, the institute outlines the program, then turns it over to the parents. Progress reports are sent at regular intervals, and return trips to the facility are scheduled only after the patient has reached a certain level of recovery. It is a three-times-a-day workout, seven days a week. If patients fail to adhere to the rigorous demands of the schedule, they are dropped from the program to make room for another who is waiting.

For the experiment to have a chance at success, the Curnutts realized, their full-time attention would be necessary. It would mean that Jerry would have to quit his job with the Department of Energy.

The Curnutts have relied on their respective retirement funds, a modest settlement granted by the courts from the estate of the man who shot their son, and aid from the Victims of Violent Crimes program since making the decision to remain at home with their son. Careful budgeting, they felt, would enable them to devote full time to the program for an estimated eighteen months before it would become financially necessary for Jerry to return to work.

Though there have been offers, the Curnutts have refused charitable help.

"We decided when we got into the program that we wouldn't look too far down the road," Jerry says. "Our approach, much like that of Kevin's, has been one day at a time."

With volunteer aid from friends throughout Arlington, the program began. Three sessions, lasting almost two hours each, were held daily. Repeatedly, the five volunteers who came to the Curnutt home gently moved Kevin's limbs through crawling and creeping motions according to Jerry Curnutt's instructions.

This is now the daily routine in the Curnutt house.

The patterning aides talk with Kevin, constantly giving encouragement. Trey's father is one of over eighty people who call themselves "Kevin's Team." So is Trey's mother. There are schoolteachers, air line pilots, bankers, and housewives among the steady stream of volunteers who arrive at the Curnutt home once, sometimes twice, a week.

"I have never been exposed to such a positive, upbeat, loving atmosphere in my life," says Kathryn Toxey, who for four years doubled as Kevin's homebound ninth and tenth-grade teacher and a member of one of the pattern groups. Today, another teacher instructs him in his high-school studies, but Ms. Toxey continues to work with the Tuesday evening patterning session.

"I think of Kevin as my own," she admits. "I love him dearly. He's got a wonderful attitude and has remained optimistic throughout all of this. To see him progress has been one of the most rewarding experiences of my life."

To the casual observer, the progress would seem minimal. Kevin still can't walk or even turn the pages of the books he enjoys reading. But he can now crawl as far as one thousand feet a day on the carpeted floor of his room. And he is able to support himself on hands and knees. Recently, he established a new "record" by moving his right knee forward thirty-six inches while on his hands and knees.

"When you understand he couldn't even hold up his head alone or move an inch along the floor when he started," says volunteer Dolly Wadlington, "then you realize the amazing progress he's made. There aren't many kids who would have the strength and courage that he has shown day after day.

"And the attitude of Jerry and Gail is incredible. They know Kevin will walk again one day, and they are devoting themselves to see that happen."

Today, Kevin Curnutt is eighteen years old. Currently a high-school senior, he is aware of the time his injury has cost him. Taking just two courses a year now, he is still four credits shy of graduation at a time when most of his friends have gone off to college.

As a result, visits from friends his own age are far fewer now. "I miss seeing a lot of my friends," he says, "but they're pretty scattered, going to different colleges and all." Troy Jackson, one of his closest buddies and a regular companion on his weekend outings, is now a student at Stephen F. Austin. "We haven't been out together in a couple of months now," Kevin says, "because he doesn't get home that much. But he calls now and then to say hello."

Some day Kevin himself hopes to be a college student, and perhaps train to become a pilot. His dreams are still intact.

And he is not bitter about the circumstances that brought him to his current station in life. "There are times when I get frustrated," he says. "Just keeping on with the program gets hard some days; particularly when I reach a plateau and don't see much improvement. But, then, things will pick up again and everything gets a lot easier.

"See, everything happens so slow—too slow. There have been times when I wondered if I was really getting any better, but then something always happened to show me that I was and I'd be okay again.

"There aren't that many mornings when I wake up and don't want to go through it all again. It hasn't been that much of a battle because I know this is what I have to do to get well. I really feel like I'm making progress now. It may take another year, maybe two. But I just have to keep telling myself to be patient."

He rarely thinks back on that January day four years ago. "I really don't remember anything about the shooting," he says. "One minute I was riding a bike and the next thing I knew, I woke up in the hospital. Thinking about it wouldn't do me any good."

On the wall of his bedroom, hanging near a collection of "gimme" hats and souvenirs given him by friends, hangs a photograph of Trey Shelton as an eighth grader. Kevin still thinks of his late friend. But the dreams that once came regularly are gone.

"I used to dream about him a lot," Kevin says. "Not nightmares, nothing scary, just dreams. I would dream that I was in the school lunchroom and see him across the room. I would go over to him and say, 'What are you doing here? I thought you were supposed to be dead.' Dreams like that. But not anymore. All that's in the past now."

Kevin Curnutt is well aware of the time, effort, and sacrifice his parents and his brother (who is now a sophomore student at the University of Texas-Arlington) have made in his behalf. "I know that Mom and Dad get frustrated at times, just like I do. But they're great. So's Kelly. Lesser people would have quit this program, or just taken off somewhere. But they believe in what we're doing, just like I do. They go to bed exhausted every night and then are ready to go again the next morning.

"And they're fun to be around. I'm lucky."

With that he falls silent for a moment, his mood becoming reflective. "Back before I got hurt," he says, "Mom and Dad used to go dancing all the time. They both love to dance. But, now, they don't have the time anymore. Sometimes I feel bad about that.

"One of the things I wish sometimes is that they could go dancing."

Some day, Jerry and Gail Curnutt may go dancing again. But not until their work is done. And Kevin is back on his feet.